This book is dedicated to the fighters. The people who fight for life, fight for love, fight for happiness and fight for their dreams! This book is to the overcomers, the survivors, the people who have fought and are now celebrating in victory and the ones who wish to overcome. To the support team of every fighter: family, friends, sometimes complete strangers and heroes. We all know it is sometimes your strength or inspiration that carries us into victory. This book is also for the ones who have lost their fights, but continue to touch our lives and encourage us every day. **~ Jenae**

Victory:

Stories From The Winners' Circle

By: Jenae Noonan

In collaboration with remarkable women sharing their stories of victory

Victory Publications can bring authors to your live event. For more information or to book an event, use the contact option at www.JenaeNoonan.com.

Who You Are and What You Want, by: Andrea Leal. *Believe you Can,* by: Amy Pond Cirelli. *All Your Thoughts in Perspective,* by: Deborah Moore and Tiffany Avans. *Pick Yourself Up and Dust Yourself Off, by*: Christine Sanchez. *Seasons,* by: Jenae Noonan and Saundra Ganem. *Compassion - Judgment Free Zone,* by: Jenae Noonan. *Learning To Dance In The Rain,* by: Jenae Noonan and Ashley Casello. *Hold Each Others' Hand On The Way Home,* by: Jenae Noonan and Ashley Casello. *"Let Go And Let God,"* by: Tiffany Avans. *Kaleidoscope - Coping with Changes,* by: Kimberly Timpe. *No Excuses,* by: Jenae Noonan and Amy M. *You are YOU,* by: Emma Borders

Photo credits: Ali Boombaye, Travis Lee

Edited by Tiffany Avans and Karla Noonan

ISBN-13: 978-0692527528

ISBN-10: 0692527524

Personal Dedications

For my husband, Ryan. There is nobody else I would rather do this journey with. Drew and Blake, you are mommy's favorites. Mom, the strongest woman I know. For Dad, Tricia, Carolyn, Jorge, Stephanie. For Mom Avans, Pappers and Sweet Grandma in heaven. For all the family and friends who have supported my marriage and family and had faith when I had none.
~ Tiffany

Steven, thank you for dancing with me in the middle of our living room at my darkest hour. Jaxson, it's because of you that mommy keeps on fighting. Dreams do come true, there IS hope, trust the Lord!
~ Christine

For my Heavenly Father who is the true author of this story, my family, friends, husband Justin and our miracle Luke William – God has placed an overabundance of love in my heart for you all.
~ Amy P.

For Sam, may he always be with me. For my sweet girl, Chanel, I hope that all trials and tribulations strengthen your beautiful soul, always. To my parents, Jeff and Judy for their perpetual support. To Frank, Sharon and Cyrus, for rising above a devastating loss with love and grace.
~ Kimberly

For God, who has given me strength to pull through. To my husband, my best friend. For the family and friends who have gone above and beyond, supporting us through the hardest time.

~ Deborah

To my husband, Jose. I couldn't imagine life without you by my side. To my precious son, Logan. Our miracle from God. You are more perfect then we ever imagined and fill our hearts with so much love.

~ Andrea

To God who has always provided a path for me, to my parents Andy and Isabel, my siblings, and my friends who have continuously encouraged me along my journey, and to anyone out there, young or old, who is hesitating jumping out. Just go for it!

~ Saundra

For my daughter, who provided me the courage to leave. To my parents, for never giving up on me, and picked me up when I fell. For my family who showed me I was never really alone. To Jenae, for being there when you did not have to be, for being my rock, getting me through this and showing me what it looks like to never give up.

~ Ashley

For you, mom

~ Amy M

For Moose

~ Love, Emma

Table of Contents

Introduction

After the release of my last book, "Fighter: Living Life Like a Champion" I sat with my best friend, whom also edited the book, and vowed never to write another. Well as you can see that statement was short lived and here we are on to the next. Upon the success of the first book I had received a lot of feedback from people sharing with me their personal stories, as well as people wanting more of my personal journey or my experiences. I began to think about what I could share that would motivate or encourage others and, with much thought, I called my best friend and told her we were writing a second book. This time I incorporated WE because I asked her to share her story. When I thought of how I could inspire others I realized that everyone has a different journey and there is no cookie cutter way to overcome seemingly impossible situations. There were just too many stories to keep to myself so I decided a compilation of stories of strength stemmed from vulnerability would be more inspiring than just my own journey.

This book is an accumulation of stories that have touched my life. These stories have inspired me never to give up, inspired me to keep pushing forward no matter what; they have empowered me and taken my breath away. These stories demonstrate what true strength looks like, what courage looks like, optimism, love, growth and many other important attributes. I hope that sharing these stories can also do the same for you. I originally intended to motivate and inspire but as the stories from these ladies were coming in, I realized this book is also about a journey of finding oneself. It's about finding your inner strength, yourself, your faith and learning to love yourself first.

The first part of this journey will help you identify what you want most out of this life, who you want to be and motivate you to stand tall and proud in that person no matter what you face. It will give you courage and hope. No matter what it is you want in this life, it is there waiting for you. The second part of the book is about finding yourself. Sometimes we are in relationships trying to grow when the most important relationship you can find is a healthy, loving relationship with yourself.

So come with me on this journey as I share with you some of the most amazing stories that I have ever heard. These ladies have poured their souls onto these papers to inspire at any stage of life. I do need a warning label that you might want to grab a box of tissue.

Who You Are and
What You Want

Anyone who has ever met a red head knows one thing for sure: we are feisty. You can tell a red head that they can't achieve something and that is the fuel they need to prove you wrong. Ok so maybe I can't speak on behalf of all the red heads on the planet, but this describes me and every single red head I have ever met. In all fairness maybe it is not just the color of our hair that makes us so stubborn or better yet, strong willed. Maybe I can't give all the credit to having the firey hair to fuel my firey personality but one thing is for sure: no one will ever get in the way of my dreams. During my motivational speeches I talk about a neck injury that I received in 2006. During a fight I took a little too much of a beating and doctors told me I would never fight again. They said I would never recover fully and any more damage to my neck could result in very scary consequences. "Find a new hobby" and "find a new job" were just a couple of the things that I was told. Like I said earlier, if you tell me I can't do something, you just gave me the fuel I need to accomplish my goal. I came back from the injury, won the national championships and went on to win a bronze medal in the world games in 2012.

Having the drive to prove people wrong isn't what pushes me. Although, it is a little more fun to smile at someone who thought I couldn't achieve my goal after achieving it. What pushes me is my "this is my life and I will do what I want to do" attitude. Too often we hear we can't do something, we can't achieve something, we don't have the resources, or that we come from the wrong back ground. These all sound like challenges to overcome and not road blocks to achieve your goals. Imagine going on a road trip in which the destination is your dream location, a paradise you have only seen in your dreams. Three hours down the road you see a sign that says that the freeway is closed ahead. Do you think, "Oh well the freeway is closed I must go home?" Do you think, "Ok lets follow the detour signs, might take a little longer but I am still going to get there," or are you thankful you have an off road vehicle, break though the barricade and drive straight onto the path you intended? Personally one of those options seems more like my speed but I am not sure how much the fines would be breaking the road block and I am not too sure how black and white prison stripes would look on me. In all honesty most of us would take the detour and eventfully get to our destination.

What is it that you want most in life and why haven't you achieved it? Your answer to the second part of that question is not road blocks stopping you from achieving your dreams. It just represents minor detours that you need to figure a way around. Sometimes it isn't the actual road block that is stopping you but it is your attitude towards it. When I saw the x-ray of my damaged neck, I could have said "Wow my neck looks bad, I must be done, you are right, I will retire," but I chose to look at that x-ray and ask, "How do I fix it? How do I make it stronger? What do I need to do to get back in the ring?" This is your life and you have the options and the resources to achieve anything and everything you want. Do not let anyone (especially yourself) tell you, you can't do it

I want to introduce you to my friend Andrea. Her story is about knowing what you want in life and not letting anyone tell you otherwise. Doctors, family and friends all seemed to have their say in how she should live her life, but at the end of the day she realized she only lives once and she will do whatever it takes to achieve what she wanted most in life. After reading her story I want you to ask yourself this question again "What is it that you want most in life and why haven't you achieved it yet?"

Andrea Leal

When I was in six grade I met the man who someday would become my husband. We were just children then and did what children do. We hung out at school and went to each other's birthday parties. In high school we went to junior homecoming together and in May of 2000, on my 19th birthday Jose asked me to be his girlfriend. I knew at that moment he was my soul mate but I wasn't sure if I was ready to "settle down." I went home to think about it. Jose and I had gone out a few times but nothing really serious. *What if I didn't accept? Would he ask me again? Was this the last chance?* I sought after my mom's advice. She had loved him from day one and she just about pushed me out the door to accept his offer. The next day he took me to the Coit Tower in San Francisco and asked me out again, and of course this time I said YES!!

We were very serious for a couple of teenagers and we knew that we would marry each other one day but not anytime soon. Six months after we started our courtship, the economy dropped and we knew now was a great opportunity to buy a house. We borrowed some of the down payment from our parents and agreed not to get engaged or get married until we paid our parents back. I was scared, *we were 19 years old, just got together, had no idea how the real world worked, and what if we broke up? What if we couldn't pay the mortgage? What if???* My excitement trumped my apprehensions and in February of 2001 we purchased our first house together. After putting a lot of blood, sweat and tears into our fixer upper we had it occupied 3 months later. We rented it out to help pay the mortgage and continued to live separately at our parent's. We were on the right track repaying our debts, everything was going as planned.

On November 25th, 2003 I went to the doctor with what I thought was flu like symptoms. He confirmed it was the flu, filled out a form for me to get blood work done, and sent me home. Before I could set foot out of his office he called me back in. He had me lay down on his doctor table and checked my spleen. I took a few deep breaths while he pressed down with his hands. I was thinking *"I'm here because I can't breathe and this guy wants to rub my belly!?"* He sent me straight to the hospital. He said it was probably nothing but since my mom was with me I didn't need to go by ambulance. I knew something was seriously wrong! *Why would I need to go by ambulance!?* As I waited to get admitted I almost passed out a few times and apparently I was so pale that the woman waiting before me let me go ahead of her. As they started running tests we had no idea what was going on. Jose had gotten there as soon as he was able. My parents waited for Jose to get there so that they could run to McDonalds for a quick bite, it was my dad's birthday dinner.

Jose and I were in the room alone, just talking to each other, and he kept reassuring me that everything was going to be ok. I was a little sacred of what the results to the test might be because how quickly they got me in, but I was young. *It couldn't be anything too bad, could it?* When the doctors walked in, they had my test results. I was diagnosed with Leukemia I couldn't believe it, I had cancer!!! *I'm only 22, I'm not supposed to have cancer, I don't want to be here. Why is this happening to me?*

To add insult to injury I was told there was nothing they could do to help me because my counts were off the charts and most likely my Leukemia was in the blast stage. I couldn't believe it! They were going to do nothing and said I was done! I couldn't believe they were just going to let me die!! So we fought for another opinion and later that afternoon I was transferred by ambulance to Stanford Hospital.

The next morning Stanford performed a bone marrow biopsy. They inserted a Catheter in my chest to start treatment and blood work; and if anything serious happened, they could get the medication to my heart faster. Later that afternoon they came in with my results. They had good news and bad news. I asked for the bad news first. The bad news was that it was indeed Leukemia and my counts were very high. They said my blood counts were the highest they had ever treated in that hospital. The good news was that it was Chronic Myeloid Leukemia (CML) which is a very slow growing cancer. In order for it to get that out of hand they said I had to have been sick for at least 2 years. I was to start treatment right away.

At the time a bone marrow transplant was the only cure and chances of survival were high with a sibling donor. My brother and my sister were both tested but neither were matches. My Oncologist recommended a new drug, that was still in the trial stage of its development, called Gleevec. It was an oral form of chemo and it was only a couple of years old so they didn't know what the long term risks were. I would have to be on this for the rest of my life and would never be able to have children. I was 22.

I didn't have many options; I wanted to live, I had a plan, and this wasn't it.

I decided to give Gleevec a try, even though there was no guarantee that it would work. It sounded better than the alternative... death. The doctor said I was young and that my chances of surviving a transplant at 22 or 32 were the same. He told me to live life to the fullest and forget that I have cancer. "Just never forget to take the chemo once a day," he said. We started treatment while I was on a heavy dose of birth control because I was due for my period. I couldn't even brush my teeth with a tooth brush because they said that if I started bleeding they wouldn't be able to stop it and I could bleed to death. I was scared. I didn't want to die and I wasn't ready to give up. I was in this to win.

I still remember my first dose as the poor nurse came in with anti-nausea medication for me to take 15 minutes prior to taking chemo. Well, me being the bad ass that I thought I was, I refused it. She had 12 different pills for me to take. I told her I didn't need anymore and that I could handle the chemo without the anti-nausea medication. Very nicely she smiled and handed over my medication with a pink bucket and with another nice smile said, "just in case". She knew what she was talking about and apparently I wasn't the bad ass that I thought I was. About 10 minutes later it all came flying out. Let's just say anti-nausea medication was definitely taken from there on out.

Doctors originally estimated that I would have to be in the hospital for at least 6 weeks until my counts came down enough to where the disease wasn't so deadly. Nine days later, after a few rounds of this new chemo and a few blood transfusions, I was going home! I went home with my treatment, anti-nausea medication, saline to flush the lines in my catheter and an overprotective mother. I was all set. My mom went home and sanitized everything (to prepare for my homecoming). I wasn't allowed out of the house because I couldn't get sick, or get any infections. My white blood counts started to drop almost immediately. I was going in every two days for follow up and after the first appointment they bumped it up to every week. After my second weekly appointment they removed my catheter and I started going monthly. My chemo was lowered from 800mg to 600mg. Things were starting to look up.

A few weeks after being sent home, on the 21st of December, Jose took me to San Francisco back to the Coit tower, (The same place he asked me out 3 ½ years ago). *Wow what's going on? I was just released from the hospital and it was mid-December and extremely cold. I was told not to leave the house. Why would Jose bring me here? Why would my mom approve?* Jose popped the question, I of course said YES!!! He had kept his word and finished paying his parents back in full. I still had a small amount left but because of my health it took a little longer then I hoped but I was able to pay them back in full the following month.

Yes! We were finally back on track. We were only 22 and we now had a lot on our plate. We decided to have a long engagement, so I could concentrate on my health and not let wedding plans overwhelm me, plus this way we also had time to save up some more money to give our home a makeover before we moved in. We set our wedding date for 2 ½ years later for July of 2006.

My white blood count was dropping pretty quickly and my chemo was reduced again to only 400mg a day and I was taking 200mg twice a day. It was about a year past being diagnosed when my numbers stopped improving; consequently, we thought treatment was no longer working. *Why did my counts stop dropping, was this bad?* My Oncologist recommend me taking the full 400mg dose at a time, and we started talking about a bone marrow transplant again. I actually had to meet with another one of their specialists. I was terrified! I didn't want a transplant. Why wasn't the medicine working?

I went back to my primary physician to discuss the day that he sent me to the hospital. He said that when he saw me walk out of his door he remembered a patient that he had over 20 years prior, a young male with the same symptoms. He sent him home with a slip for blood work. The young man waited a few weeks to get his blood work done, and by the time the doctor received the results he called the young man to go to the hospital ASAP. The young man didn't make it. His death wasn't in vain. I believe that young man helped save my life because if I had walked out that door with what we all thought was the flu that could have been my fate too.

      Two and a half years came and went since the terrifying diagnosis and my counts were finally normal. On July 29, 2006 just like we planned, before God, our friends and family, my soul mate became my husband. We got to grow up together... Now we get to grow old together. A few years passed where everything was perfect. We completely remodeled our house over time and made it into our home. But our home was empty and the feeling of wanting a family was really heavy. At the time the only options we knew of was adoption or surrogacy or risk my life by going off my chemo and try myself, or just give up my desire to become a mother.

      In 2008, we considered our options but my Oncologist gave me the red light to stop treatment and carry the baby myself. He also gave me the red light to stop treatment temporarily for the surrogate route. *I can't carry the baby full term, and we can't have a baby via surrogate and we weren't ready to adopt yet. What were we going to do?* I was frustrated. I felt healthy since my counts had been undetectable for a few years now, but my doctor said NO, so my husband said NO! I was crushed; all I know was that I wanted to be a mom!!

      I started researching for hours, days, weeks and months on end to determine a plan. What should we do? I came across an article about another young CML patient (she was a writer for *Glamour* magazine) who had gone off treatment to have her baby and I thought: if she could do it why can't I? Her younger sister was a match, so she had plan B ready. Again neither of my siblings is a match so I had no plan B. She eventually gave birth to a handsome little boy, and both mom and baby were healthy (she has had two more children since then). I still refused to give up and continued researching the pros and cons of all our options. One of her posts about having a baby after cancer, and it was about yet another young lady, named Jen, who was also diagnosed with CML. Jen had decided to go the surrogate route and she was blessed with twins!!!

The surrogate route seemed like the best route for me, so against my doctors' opinion, we moved forward. I got in contact with Jen. She lived nearby, in Oakland, California. To find a random person online in the same shoes I was who lives less than an hour away felt like fate! We corresponded on the phone and online for about a year. As fate would have it, she went to Stanford too!! With all the similarities there was no doubt in my mind we were facing the right direction. She told me that her Oncologist at Stanford and her fertility doctor at UCSF worked together as a team throughout the whole process!

It's now 2011, eight years since being dealt the cancer card and now six years of marriage. What did I do? I did what any other women in my shoes would do; I ditched my Oncologist and switched to one who would support my strong desire to be a mother. We met with my new doctor and he was on board with me stopping treatment just long enough for fertility treatments. As soon as we implanted into our surrogate I would resume treatment right away. *Deal, I will take it!*

New Year's resolution 2012: "Let's have a baby." We scheduled our first appointment with our fertility specialist in February of 2012 in which Jose and I both got tested. My follicles were on the low side but hubby looked great, and we only need one right? We moved forward. Jen and I became friends and since Oakland is so close to San Francisco she invited us over for dinner after our appointment. After a couple years of corresponding, we met each other in person for the first time. After dinner, Jose and I discussed the surrogate process with Jen and her husband. They had so much useful information. What a blessing! Shortly after, we found a surrogate!!

Jen and I met for lunch with my surrogate and the mother of the child she had recently given birth too. We hit it off and in April we all joined the "Be A Match" walk where our husbands met for the first time, and they also hit it off. I started looking for attorneys and an insurance company that will cover a surrogate mother. Done! Both parties had their evolutions done by our attorneys and we all got blood work done to verify we didn't have any disease that could get passed on to the baby. All four of us passed. We found our surrogate, had my Oncologist and fertility specialist working together, found our attorneys, one to represent us and another one to represent our surrogate, and I found her a medical plan. This is not how I imagined I would have kids but I was so excited we were finally going to have a baby!!

Our surrogate went on birth control, so we could synchronize our cycles and ovulate simultaneously. I could almost taste the sweet baby that would bless our family. After working together for about eight months, our surrogate and I met for lunch. We started discussing the contract and she did a huge 180. Even though we agreed to pay her more than most surrogates generate, she was suddenly demanding more money plus a gym membership, massages, a housekeeper and someone to help her care for her kids (even though she was a stay at home mom and her parents lived with her family). I felt so uncomfortable that I came home crying and I told Jose what happen. We asked ourselves, "if we feel uncomfortable with her, how would we feel with her carrying our baby?"

Jose thought it was a good idea for the four of us to meet in person again, and get this all figured out. I called our attorney, told her what happened, and to put our contract agreement on hold until we can come to an agreement. One of the new terms the surrogate wanted in our agreement was actually fraudulent and our attorney said if we decided to use her as our surrogate she would no longer represent us. As much as we wanted to be parents, we decided it was best to walk away. Jose wanted to start over and find a new surrogate but the emotional roller coaster left me feeling drained, and I decided to give it a break.

In December of 2012 I had my appointment at Stanford. I told my doctor what had happened and he told me that I had other options. *Do tell doc!* He told me that I was in a hematologic response for the past two years; he was willing to monitor me monthly if I was willing to go off of treatment myself. It would be a huge risk but I had faith. Effective immediately it was good bye Gleevec and hello Operation Make a Baby. Without hesitation, I stopped treatment, and started getting monitored monthly. Let the baby making games begin!

After an eight month break from Gleevec and actively trying to conceive, in August of 2013, my white blood counts started to rise, and I wasn't pregnant yet. Conceiving was not going to be as easy as I had thought. I decided it was in my best interest to start treatment again. Once the blood count was back down I went off the treatment and back on the baby making plan. We continued trying to have a baby and I was taking pregnancy tests more often so that if it turned up positive, I could stop treatment immediately. I was losing hope. Maybe it wasn't meant for me to be a mother. In March of 2014, I had an HSG test done to see if my fallopian tubes were clear. Everything looked great and there was no known reason why this wasn't working for us. In May I had given up hope and started setting up appointments for help, after 17 months of trying. It was time for some help in the fertility department. On May 19th I stopped treatment. I don't know why, but I did; I got a bad gut feeling every time I would put that pill in my hand, so I would just put it back in the bottle. I had no good reason to stop treatment other than a gut feeling.

Almost 18 months after making my decision to have a baby, I peed on a stick (like I did every day for a week every month for the last 18 months) and on June 3rd, 2014, there was the slightest colored little second line. *Wait, can this be? Can I actually be pregnant?* I showed Jose and he said it was false, "that line is so light we were imagining it's there." Light or not, it was there. The next morning I took another test, and again very light, and I went to work. Could I really just be imagining this? Who was I kidding; I couldn't focus while at work so I lied and said I had a headache one hour into my shift, and came home and tested with four different tests. They all came back positive so I called my primary doctor and she got me in that day for blood work. *It's positive!!! I'm pregnant!!!* When I told Jose I didn't get the reaction I was hoping for. He gave me a hug and said "cool." I was heartbroken! I knew that this wasn't his first option as he was afraid for me being off my life-saving Gleevec and wanted to go the surrogate route, but still!!! He didn't start showing excitement until 24 weeks in, knowing that if something went wrong, the baby out and I would both have a greater chance of survival. After eight years of being told I could never have children, two more years being on the path of using a surrogate and another year and a half of trying to conceive naturally, we were finally pregnant.

By the grace of God I was able to carry our son full term. Every kick, every ultrasound, every heartbeat and every moment of my pregnancy was a true gift. Our lives forever changed on February 5th, 2015. After 37 hours of labor at 4:01pm, I gave birth to the most precious little boy via C-section. He was 8lbs 9oz and 20.5 inches long of pure perfection!! We now experience a joy I never knew existed and I was pleasantly surprised to see Jose jump into daddy mode. We couldn't be any happier! Every single moment with our little man was so worth the battle. Jose always said we were a family before Logan but I did not feel that we were a family until the day Logan was born.

Fast forward seven months and we are doing great. I was able to stay off treatment to breastfeed but due to a rise in my white blood counts, I am now back on treatment. On the weekends we like to bring Logan into bed with us in the morning and just stare at him and play with him. We are amazed at all the new things he does, trying to roll over, his fake cough for attention, trying different foods, and don't even get me started on the baby giggles. Jose and I have always tackled life as a team and it is no different as our new family of three. I didn't think I could possibly love my husband anymore until he became the father of my son. He sings to him, plays with him, talks to him, and even changes diapers! We are looking forward to this journey again and are hoping to give our son a sibling. I did agree with my Oncologist that I would go back on my life saving-drugs for a year before we try for miracle #2. Until then, I get to cherish so many heart melting moments in our household right now and can't imagine living my life any other way.

Believe

Andrea's story was a great example of how to go after what you want in life no matter what road blocks cross your path. Along with having the will to do whatever it takes to achieve your dream, you need to believe you can. Sounds like a simple concept but sometimes when I am working with people who want to achieve their dreams, they tell me all the obstacles they might face. In telling me this, they give themselves a trap door. Meaning, they will tell me why they might fail and when things get hard they say "I guess I was right. This is why I failed." You will fail 100% of the time when you think you will, because you are telling yourself you are going to.

One thing I have yet to achieve in my life time is having a successful relationship. Dating is the worst and for whatever reason very difficult for me and here is where I fail 100% of the time because I think I will fail. I always think the reason a person isn't texting me is because they don't want to talk to me. I want to hang out with that person but I won't text them because of my belief that if they wanted to spend time with me, they would text me. Because of my thinking that I was going to fail that night spending time with that individual, I succeeded in failing. I don't know what the outcome would be if I tried but I know I will succeed in failing 100% of the time if I believe I will. Growing up I played soccer and my coach would say, "you miss 100% of the shots you don't take." You won't make the shot if you don't take it. You won't take the shot if you don't believe you'll make it.

When I was working on rehabbing my neck, I was doing all the things that I was told would strengthen it. I told myself that these exercises were going to be what fixed my neck and what would put me back on the road I wanted to be on. Maybe not the exact road but on a road that would lead to my desired destination. I never doubted that maybe these exercises wouldn't work, or thought that maybe my neck won't be strong enough. If I had those thoughts would I have gotten back in the ring? If I thought that my neck wasn't strong enough to step back in the ring would I have won a national championship? Thinking "nothing is going to stop me" and" I can and will achieve my goals" are the two affirmations you need, in order to be unstoppable. Some people find strength in the bible verse "I can do all things through Christ who strengthens me" (Phil 4:13). This verse allows them to say I may not have the strength but I know He does and in

Him I can do this. There is also a verse in Matthew 17:20 that says, "Truly I tell you, if you have faith as small as a mustard seed, you can say to this mountain, 'Move from here to there,' and it will move. Nothing will be impossible for you. With faith of a mustard seed you can move mountains." How much more can you do when you do not let an ounce of doubt enter your mind? The mind is a powerful thing. Know exactly what you want. Don't let anything get in your way and with all your heart and faith know that you can and will achieve your dream.

In this next story Amy knew what she wanted and wasn't going to let anything get in her way, but it was faith, tenacity and determination that got her there. Like Andrea, there were so many times where it seemed like her dreams were not going to happen. Amy pushes towards her goal with faith in God leading the way, and with faith that she can and will achieve it.

Amy Pond Cirelli

Looking back I always thought I would have kids. If someone had asked me in high school what I thought my life would look like my answer was that I would be "married by 22 and have a couple of kids by the time I was 25. Then, obviously, I would live happily ever after with my husband." Thinking back on that memory now makes me laugh so hard that tears stream down my face. As you can imagine that is not exactly the way things worked out.

Let's start at the beginning shall we? I was incredibly blessed to meet and fall in love with my husband in high school. We were engaged to be married in June of 2007 and were married in October of 2008, making it exactly seven years and seven months from the start of our relationship to marriage. Of all of the important conversations you have leading up to marriage there was one that always stuck with me and, of course, it revolved around kids and a family.

When asked by our pastor in one of the counseling sessions about family, we had both said that we didn't know if we ever wanted kids. What?! I know... looking back, the thought was surprising to me too. However, I was so amazed by the love that God gave me for this incredible man, that I just knew that kids or no kids he was my family and that it wasn't something that would ever be a "deal breaker". This just goes to show how God is always working in absolutely everything.

Fast forward to January of 2011 when talks of a family began to really creep back into conversations in a very real way. My best friend had just had her son and I was smitten to say the least. Every time I held him I just never wanted to give him back. So by March of 2011, we were officially trying to have a baby. Or if you would have asked us, we were just leaving it up to God, and not taking any preventative measures.

With excitement, I threw my pill away and headed to Target to purchase some pre-natal vitamins because I read that you should take them before you are ever pregnant and I wanted to be on top of things. We never told our family about our new plans because the idea of putting pressure on such a beautiful thing just didn't feel right; and to be honest, having this little secret with just my husband was thrilling.

In April of 2011 we headed to the east coast with my parents to fulfill one of my many dreams, to run the Boston Marathon. It was an incredible trip, and an interesting one, trying to hide my pre-natal vitamins and try for a baby while on vacation with my parents. Unfortunately, the month of April didn't lead to a positive pregnancy test and while we were leaving it up to God I was beginning to get impatient. I thought that this was supposed to be easy. I mean, seriously... people got pregnant on accident and weren't we always told that it only took one time? What a sham!

May and June weren't much better so with the blessing of my husband, I headed to the store to purchase my first ovulation test. July was going to be the month if I had anything to say about it and it was. In August of 2011, we got our very first positive home pregnancy test! To say we were excited was an understatement. However, very quickly reality set in and a bit of fear crept in too. We just couldn't believe that this was really happening. As expected the first doctor's appointment was routine and we got the official congratulations from the doctor. We had decided not to tell anyone quite yet, which really meant that we only told our few closest friends.

It wasn't more than a week later I noticed that I was spotting. It wasn't much and it was brown, but I called the doctor right away. I was assured that it was completely normal. So naturally, I prayed about it and didn't give it much thought. The next week we went in for our very first ultrasound. We weren't quite six weeks yet, so I knew not to expect to see much but we were excited none the less. Unfortunately the experience wasn't exactly what I had expected because they wouldn't even let my husband in the room. I didn't understand, but they said that they don't let the husbands in that early. So I headed in while he waited patiently. The appointment was quick and we left with our very first photo and an estimated due date of April 21, 2012. Time to share the news with our parents!

So under the disguise of sharing photos from our east coast trip and the marathon, we invited my parents out to lunch. We had brought photos with us, and slipped the ultrasound photo in between them to surprise them. The surprise worked and I will never forget the excitement and tears of that joyful day! Next we met with my husband's parents and aunt and shared the good news. We had just been on a family vacation with them and wanted to give them thank you cards. In the card we shared that they would be grandparents.

The next week, after quite a long week at work, I had a follow up ultrasound. By now the spotting had stopped and I went to the appointment on my own. I knew they wouldn't let my husband back with me so we just thought we would spend the day together after. I remember the appointment like it was yesterday because it was just so odd. The technician never let me see the screen, took tons of photos, and asked me to stay still and hold my breath. Looking back I know that she was searching for a heartbeat, one that she would never find.

I left the appointment upset, but headed home trying to be positive and praying for good news. In order to not sit around and wait for the doctor to call, we headed to Sam's Club to get some things done. We had just gotten out of the car when my phone rang and we got the news. I will never forget dropping my purse on the asphalt, crying tears that came from so deep I didn't know where they were really coming from and telling my husband that I was done. I didn't want to have a baby anymore, my heart just hurt too badly.

Like true adults, I said we should just get groceries because we were already there. Then we headed home and just hibernated in bed. I felt like I just couldn't move. Telling our friends and family was hard. I remember telling my mother then saying that I couldn't tell anyone else. In all honesty, the rest of that day was a total blur. I just know that my husband took care of telling his mother.

The next day at work I got a call from my doctor and she explained what I should expect and we set a follow up appointment. Well unfortunately for me, my brain and emotions understood that I had a miscarriage, but my body did not. After a little more than a week with no indication of an impending bleed my doctor scheduled a D&C. The procedure itself wasn't painful, but I just felt empty. All of my excitement and hopes for a family were gone and all I felt was failure and pain. I wracked my brain for what I had done wrong and spent many months not forgiving myself for this imaginary wrong doing. I understood that these things happened, but I didn't know anyone whom it had ever happened to, so I thought it must have been me. I spent a lot of time talking to God and just asking why? I never got an answer, but I leaned on Him.

In a follow up appointment with my doctor, she wanted to run some tests and at this time we found out that I had hypothyroidism, which can be a factor in miscarriage. I was disappointed, but happy to have something I could do. Just one pill, daily for the rest of my life? No big deal!

After a lot of conversation, and a little time, we decided that we did still want a child and if it was as easy as getting my thyroid in order then we were in. We didn't officially start trying again until January of 2012. Mentally and physically I just wasn't ready until then.

The year of 2012 just lead to heartbreak with month after month of disappointment. Each month would initially start out with excitement and expectation only to leave me wondering why. We had spent a fortune on ovulation tests, pregnancy tests, and had one quite painful test where they shot dye into my uterus to see if my tubes were blocked – luckily for me my one tube was fine and the other "might" be blocked. Here we are, not even 30 years old yet and have tried for another year with absolutely no results. To say that 2012 took everything out of me would be a vast understatement. Don't get me wrong, many wonderful things happened in other areas of life but like with many obstacles in life I couldn't see further than a few feet ahead.

At this point my doctor said that there wasn't really anything else that she could do for us. She recommended us to a fertility clinic, the same one that she had used and we made an appointment. I mean, if it was good enough for my doctor to go to, I figured it was good enough for me.

We met Dr. A for the very first time in January of 2013. He was incredibly nice, very knowledgeable and super blunt. After reviewing the 11 page history we submitted before the appointment, he said he thought that we were being impatient and with time we would probably get pregnant on our own. Thinking back on that initial appointment now makes me shrug my shoulders and laugh a bit. With all of the financial and physical costs that we would endure in the following years, I can still appreciate his honesty. In fact, I have to say that is truly one of the things I always liked the most. Fortunately, for us we knew that we were done trying on our own and decided to move forward with his course of treatment. Step one.... medicated cycles with timed intercourse. Sounds romantic, huh?? However, we tackled this just like everything else thus far, as a team.

Prior to this we hadn't been regular church goers. We believed in God, prayed and leaned on Him, but to say that we were in a growing relationship where we sought after God in a meaningful way would have been untrue. As we stepped out onto the waters and into this journey, we found that God had softened our hearts and changed us. We began going to church on a regular basis and I had purchased my first devotional and began reading daily. Our team had a defined leader and that was and is God.

We attempted medicated cycles, which are just as romantic as they sound. I mean who really wants to get a shot in the hip before bed, and then have to wake up before the birds to be "romantic" before work. I love my husband VERY much, but seriously neither one of us was even really awake! After three unsuccessful medicated cycles the doctor recommended we moved on to our first inter uterine insemination or IUI. Here, they monitor each cycle closely, trigger your ovulation with medication, and actually inseminate you placing everything right where it should be. No guessing. We reached out to family and only a few select friends and asked for prayer. At this point I really didn't want to share with a lot of people what we were doing. I wasn't ashamed, but I felt like a failure and just didn't want anyone to know how hard this was. Especially, because it seemed like it was just hard for me.

Everywhere I looked I would see pregnant people. It seemed like everyone, including my friends, were getting pregnant and it just wouldn't happen for me. Now I must say I have never been a fan of tears, probably because I don't like feeling that exposed, but also because for some reason they always made me feel weak. Most of the tears that emerged during this time happened in secret. It was only when I was by myself that I would really look and ask myself, *what is wrong with me? Would I be that bad of a mother that I just shouldn't be allowed to have a child? Or why was everyone else worthy and not me?* Even the teenager walking around the Fair with her boyfriend was pregnant and here I am with an empty bedroom fit for a nursery, love in my heart, and a desire to be a mother and I couldn't make this happen even with medical intervention. My levels of hope and positivity were plummeting daily.

After two unsuccessful IUI's, and another few months of tears that I never really wanted to let out, we took a break and the next month my doctor performed a laparoscopy in September 2013. He wanted to see what was going on in my uterus. It wasn't until after the procedure showed that my uterus was "text book" that I found out he was expecting to have to remove a tube or

something. He just couldn't figure out what the problem was.
Now I see that it just wasn't time yet. God had more to do. He was
refining my heart daily, making me more compassionate to others
going through any and all struggles, reminding me to lean on Him
and not my own understanding and slowly re-filling my soul with
hope.

In October, I was feeling really good. I had decided that
there wasn't anything wrong with me. I mean, clearly, the surgery
didn't show anything, so I was determined to go forward and stop
beating myself up. We decided to have a month off from the
fertility clinic and just enjoy each other. Well, much to our
surprise on November 21st, 2013 we got a positive pregnancy test!
We were over the moon!!! What an incredible blessing. This time
we shared with our family and close friends right away. If we had
learned anything from the last time it was that we needed prayer
and support from the very beginning. And boy was the prayer and
support amazing. To see how our family had grown with us
during this time and how they had grown individually in their
relationship with God was just incredible to see.

We called Dr. A and gave him the news. They scheduled us
for an ultrasound on December 10th, but it wasn't more than a
week later that I began spotting again. Knowing what this meant
for the fate of my baby the last time, to say that I was worried
would be an understatement. We continued to pray and give it to
God but worry encompassed my thoughts daily. The doctor

scheduled a round of blood tests to check my levels and to our surprise my levels were still rising like they should. The night before the ultrasound I told my husband that I didn't think the news would be good and asked him what he thought we should do.

True to his nature, he said we just needed to see what God had for us. On ultrasound day, I read my devotional in the morning and I remember that it was an entire page on hope. I tried to be hopeful; however, during the ultrasound I fully expected for the doctor to give us the bad news. When he said, "there is the heartbeat" my heart swelled to a size that could barely fit in my chest! We couldn't believe it. Our prayers had been answered! We left that day praising God for this miracle and couldn't stop listening to the recording of the heartbeat that we left the doctors with.

The next two weeks were routine. The spotting had stopped, prayers and time with God had continued and all seemed wonderful with the world. I mean how could it not be? God had blessed me with an incredible husband and now a growing baby.

We went to our next ultrasound on December 23d. The excitement was palpable. We just wanted to see our baby again and hear that precious sound of its beautiful heartbeat, but that wasn't part of God's plan for us. Unfortunately, the news wasn't good and at just under 10 weeks we had lost baby number two.

We were devastated. I was both teary eyed and in shock at the very same time and my husband had to literally hold my waist up as we left. I knew the routine from the last time, but luckily this time by blood work indicated that I could expect my body to take care of everything on its own. It would just take a few weeks.

Somehow we made it through the holidays. To be honest I really don't know how. The hope that was once re-filling in me had once again been drained from my body and I was like an empty shell. Luckily for me, my offices at work close the week before Christmas until just after the New Year so I was able to do just what I wanted – be mad at God and stay in bed for as long as I wanted. So I did just that. I was so upset I remember telling God that I loved him very much, but I was mad and that we weren't on speaking terms. Even as I write that I laugh at how I spoke to my father. I mean seriously Amy?! When I should have leaned on Him and sought Him to fill the hole and for ultimate healing, I found my 12 year old self and told Him that I wasn't going to talk to him.

Luckily, I returned to my 30 year old self in time for New Year's and rang in 2014 on speaking terms with God. Just in time for the worst physical and emotional pain that I have ever experienced because of course, it would happen on New Year's Eve. About a month prior, my family and I got tickets to a New Year's Eve party with dinner, drinks and dancing and of course the tickets were not refundable. So when my body officially started to miscarry that day I thought I could still suck it up and go, and I did.

What I didn't expect was for everything with my body to happen so fast. I spent 90 percent of the night in the bathroom doubling over in pain. I imagine the pain of childbirth is much worse, but at least you get to hold your baby in your arms after. This just left me in pain and feeling empty again. But in my true fashion, I kept my feelings inside and I am in many of the NYE photos smiling and trying to hide the fact that on the inside I felt like I was falling apart.

So here we are in January of 2014, a year after our very first visit, sitting in Dr. A's office yet again. This time to order blood testing to see what is going on. Of all of the tests the big one was the karyotyping. This one tests for chromosomal disorders that can potentially cause problems. Naturally, I checked the internet and found that most people who do these tests never actually get an answer. So I decided that I was going to stay off the internet and just give it to God, for real this time. No worrying.

In February, we were back in Dr. A's office to find out that I had a balanced translocation in chromosomes numbers two and nine, as well as a blood clotting disorder and problem processing folic acid. My husband on the other hand is Superman! While I remember not wanting anything to be wrong with him, I wouldn't wish that on anyone, I also didn't want it to be me. My husband had married a dud. I was literally the failure that I thought I was, and all of this really was my fault. I was devastated but still tried to keep a brave face in the doctor's office. I remember asking my husband if he would still have married me knowing what he knew now. I mean, who would really want to endure the last few years of pain and loss if they knew they could avoid it? But he said yes, this wasn't a deal breaker and never was going to be. Oh how God had been weaving all of this together!

The doctor gave us our options, IVF with pre-genetic testing to ensure that any embryos implanted were chromosomally normal or to continue trying on our own because eventually it could happen for us, with the key word being, eventually. Statistically, one in every four of my eggs should be normal, so while it could take a while and result in loss it really just depended on what our hearts could take.

Luckily, you don't have to make a decision on the spot. We headed home and discussed it with our family and looked at our finances. I have to say that I never really saw myself doing IVF. It always just seemed so expensive, and why not just adopt? But here we were looking at the options in front of us and IVF was it. For some reason it just felt right and because God had been leading our finances even when we weren't paying any attention and we took out what we now refer to as the "baby loan".

In March of 2014 we began our very first round of IVF. I don't think we had any idea what we were really in for, but we were confident that this is where we needed to be. My husband was truly a rock through everything. He administered many injections, laughed with me at being a chemist at home, and rubbed the injection sites so that they wouldn't hurt so badly. After a month and a half of injections we had the egg retrieval in April and we got eight eggs. All fertilized and on day three were looking good. I was so excited! It felt like finally my body was doing something right. I had no doubt that one of those precious embryos would be our baby. *I mean, this has to be it, how much more could we endure?* On day five they would be testing the embryos and on day six they would implant and I was ready. Unfortunately, by day five we had no remaining embryos they had all "arrested" or in my eyes had died. I just didn't understand, my body had failed me again. Statistically, there should have been at least two that were good, but God doesn't work in statistics, He works in miracles.

When we decided to move forward with IVF we had wisely chosen the two round option. It just seemed like too much pressure to put all of our eggs in one round, so to speak. So after a month off, we started round two in June. With a lot of prayer we had thought that this was probably going to be it. We just didn't know how much more we could really take, but hoped that we wouldn't have to find out. This time the medication was adjusted and I was a human pin cushion. On the day of the egg retrieval, they retrieved 12 eggs and we began the process of doctor updates on our precious embryos every other day. By day four I had gotten a call that there were four embryos but that they didn't look like they were going to be ready for genetic testing. I tried not to cry as I asked the head nurse if that meant they were slowing down and would probably arrest. She said she was praying for us, and that she just didn't know.

How could we be in this place again? It was beyond what I could comprehend. I called my husband to let him know and returned to my desk at work trying to hold back the tears and hold on to hope. That night I didn't want to make dinner and really just wanted to have a relaxing evening and a drink. So we headed out to dinner and I asked my husband what we were going to do. I felt like I needed a plan, just something that could give me at least an illusion of control. However, that is not the man I married. He wisely told me that we should just wait until the next day and see what happened, that God had a plan.

The next day at work I get a call from the head nurse that two of the embryos were headed out for genetic testing and we would hear something the next day, but at this point if there was a good one it would need to be frozen! I was speechless and jumping up and down in my office. I immediately called my husband at work and our family to share the news and to ask for prayer. God had been listening all along and there was still a chance. When all seemed hopeless God provided us with His ultimate hope. That Friday gave us our first good phone call from the doctor's office... We had one normal embryo!

Our perfect little miracle embryo was frozen and we decided to wait until what we considered was the optimum time to transfer. With July through September being the busiest and most stressful months for me at work and my sister getting married out of town in October, we thought that a November transfer would be best. This time we weren't going to do anything alone, at this point only our immediate family and very close friends were by our side and it was time to share with everyone.

My mother contacted the elders at the church and we held a prayer night at our house. I was overwhelmed with the love of our family and friends and the power of prayer that night and every moment since. For the first time I really understood what it meant to give it to God and to let Him have the spotlight. It was His time to shine. No hiding my prayers. I would continue to love and worship God no matter what happened.

On November 9th, Dr. A transferred our miracle embryo, my husband took care of me for three full days of mandatory bed rest, and we began the 12 day wait to find out if God had, indeed, blessed us with the miracle we had been praying for. On November 21st, exactly one year from the last positive pregnancy test we headed in to have my blood drawn. We had decided not to take a test at home, but to just follow the instructions given and wait. Believe it or not this was actually easier than I thought it would be. After years of negative pregnancy tests, I was starting to feel like they were broken anyhow. Also, I knew that if it was positive I would have forever to be grateful and excited, but if it was negative I didn't want to know any sooner then I needed to. Somehow, I finally felt a sense of peace, just knowing that no matter what, everything would be ok. My husband loved me and God had a plan.

After the doctor, we both headed to work and I held tightly to my cell phone. I even took it with me to the bathroom! No matter what the news was, I didn't want to miss a phone call from the doctors, and just before noon they called and they asked me to hold for a moment. The next thing I knew I was on speaker with all of the nurses we had worked with because they all wanted to be a part of telling me I was pregnant! Even writing that now brings me to tears. Happy tears because these incredible people were so excited for us that they all wanted to be a part of this special moment. I immediately called my husband at work to give him the good news and when I got off the phone I dropped to my knees. God gave us a miracle! Not just for our eyes but for everyone to see and He deserves all of the praise!

Our doctor's appointments all lined up just like they had with our pregnancy the year before, December 10th and December 23rd but this time they were different. They all showed the miracle that God was knitting together and we were so excited to share it with our family and friends! We held off on social media announcement, but shared our joy with everyone who had been on this journey with us.

You would think that after experiencing this miracle that I wouldn't worry or be anxious. However, that is the furthest from the truth. In fact, around weeks five and six I was a wreck every time I went to the bathroom thinking that I would have the same heartbreaking experience as before. At every doctor's appointment I would be a wreck until I heard the heartbeat and the doctor said that everything was going the way it should. God is working in me every day. I worry and I give it to Him. I pray daily for the healthy, safe and full term delivery of His miracle and am reminded that this isn't my child but His. He has a plan for him or her just like He has a plan for me.

We waited almost 18 weeks to make the big announcement to the world. It took a lot of prayer to figure out just how and when to do it, and to be honest I was afraid. There was a time when I actually considered just waiting until the baby was born so we could send out a birth announcement.

Now, as I sit here eight months pregnant, I am in awe of this experience and everything that God has done and continues to do. I am beyond excited to meet this person that God has created and to hold him or her in my arms. I pray daily that he or she would come to know God, be saved and bear fruit for His kingdom, that we would be the parents He desires us to be and that as a family we would shine His light and share His love with everyone. I pray these prayers knowing that they are how I desire to measure success and how I want to enter into every season of life.

I see with new eyes and have a hope that I never knew existed. I worship an incredible God who loves to give gifts to his children, but also loves us enough to mold and shape us no matter how it hurts to be refined in the fire. I am forever grateful for the prayers of everyone, for finally having the courage to share with others and how God used this experience to show He is the miracle worker.

To say the last eight months have been easy would be a lie. I continue to grow every day, leaning on God in ways I never had before. He has calmed my anxious heart and continued to knit this baby together every day. I still get anxious but find so much comfort in knowing that God is here. He is listening and He has blessed me with an incredible group of people who love, support and pray for me and this baby every day. I am grateful for all of the people that God has used during this experience and how my relationships with them have grown and changed. I am happy to share with them and share my life in a much more meaningful way and I can honestly say that I no longer feel like a failure. God doesn't make failures, He made me just the way He had planned.

It has also been amazing to see how He has used this experience to change others. I have watched relationships mend, and others see God in a new way. I always thought miracles were just things of the bible. I never thought I would be part of one, but here I sit. I worship a God who doesn't work in statistics but works in miracles and I will take the hope that this miracle has given me into every season of life so that I will always remember that with God, nothing is hopeless.

All Your Thoughts
In Perspective

I cannot illustrate the power of perspective more than in the story I am about to share with you. Quality of life is but a culmination of how you perceive it. Many unexpected events happen in life; control is only an illusion. Everything that *happens to you* can be perceived as negative or positive. It's a pretty simple concept but a very powerful one once you realize you have control over it. You get to control how you perceive each situation you encounter. You have the power to choose to live a positive life or a negative life.

Perception is a choice. You choose what you see. Two people are stuck in the same traffic jam. Monica sits in her car and lets her blood pressure increase. In her eyes she's not going as fast as she would like. She may be late to work and she is miserable and are not experiencing life in a positive way. The next car over is Joe, who sees the traffic as just slow moving. He realizes he can't control it and he will spend that extra time listening to his favorite album and enjoy his morning coffee. He is choosing to live in the light instead of the stress over what he currently has no control. Two people in the same situation: one person let the negativity fester and thrive, the other has made the choice to roll with the punches and take Queen Elsa's advise and "Let it go!"

Another example is two people are laid off from a company experiencing financial distress. Jane thinks that this could be the best thing that happened to her and she can now focus on pursuing a dream job or build the company she has always wanted to build. She chooses to toast to new beginnings and endless opportunity with this new chapter. John sits in his car festering in the pity party *thinking how will I find another job? How am I going to pay the rent? Now what am I going to do? When am I going to get a break? Life could not possibly get any worse!* He hated his job anyways but is now magnifying the negative mind set and, much like the concept in *The Secret,* is sending a ripple of negativity out into the world.

In every situation we face we are given our own freedom of how we perceive the situation. We can chose to walk into the light and see it for the positive experience we are looking for or we can walk to the darkness and get angry and have negative feelings towards the situation. You get to make the choice to live a happy positive life or a grumpy negative one. I personally hate the fact that I am extremely single (at the moment) and have to catch myself choosing to experience this loneliness in a negative way.

Yes it hurts sometimes. Yes I am down sometimes but I am aware that although I can't change the situation I can change how I perceive it. I can look at this situation as woe is me or I can embrace the free time to do what I want, when I want. One of those feeling is a downer and energy draining; the other is motivating and energizing. Every day I get to choose how I feel about where I am in life. I get to choose how I experience life. I choose to stay positive because it's just a better feeling. What you think about you will find. If you want to find more happy moments, think more happy thoughts. What you seek you will find. Sounds biblical, but it is true, if you constantly are looking for the negative, you will find the negative, if you look for positive, you will find positive.

This next story is written by a remarkable woman who, despite unimaginable trials, has the most beautiful perspective and zest for life than anyone I have ever met. When you see her smile, you lose site that she is missing anything and somehow appears to be more complete in spirit than many who have more than she.

Deborah Moore

All my life has been an adventure. I grew up in a full house with two loving parents, three sisters and five brothers. There was never a dull moment. I spent a lot of time with the boys in the house climbing trees, playing Tonka trucks and hide n seek. Every year we vacationed at Lake Havasu where we camped and boated. I became a life guard in high school and a water safety instructor and that was my passion for over thirty five years. I met Jon in college bible studies. We became good friends and our courtship led to a lifetime commitment to each other. Shortly after we were married, our family grew and we were blessed with a son and then a daughter, making our little family complete. This is the "once upon a time" of my bittersweet and blessed adventure.

One of many memorable points on my adventure was my run-in with breast cancer. I was 45 years old at the time and of all the treatment options, I chose to give up "the girls". I decided against radiation, chemo and Tomoxifin and moved forward with a bilateral mastectomy and reconstruction. It was it all done in one very invasive surgery. Recovery was challenging but I was back to swimming my laps and playing racquetball a year later. In this experience, I saw the ugliness of cancer's destruction and also the beauty of how God can make us stronger through the trials.

Cancer made me think about death more than I would have liked to. Filling out an advance directive was a huge eye opener for me, indicating on paper, what my wishes were in the event that I couldn't speak for myself. I had to decide whether or not I wanted to be resuscitated should I become non-responsive and what medical interventions I was comfortable with in the event that I couldn't breathe on my own. No one likes to discuss death in reference to themselves or anyone else in their lives. It is never fun to attend funerals or accept the inevitable truth that our body will be all that remains one day. We tend to fear death and live our life as though it will never happen to us, as though we are somehow invincible. My fear grew into acceptance knowing that

Jesus died for me because He loved me. It was in those moments of accepting that it could happen during my cancer experience that I knew where I would go after death and would submit my life to God's purpose and perfect will for me for the rest of my days. Looking back, I forget about breast cancer most of the time, because that experience was easy compared to some of the challenges that followed.

I was working at Liberty Elementary the year my life-changing illness occurred. I loved my job as a Health Technician. I enjoyed working with the children and their parents and the staff was a truly great team to work with. On December 23rd, 2008, I was preparing for a two week Christmas break, one of the many perks I got working at the school. I was getting our home ready to celebrate the birth of Jesus. I was tired and I over did it, as all of us mothers tend to do. I went to bed and woke up with a high fever. I thought I had food poisoning or the flu. Within twenty-four hours I felt like fainting and ended up in the emergency room. Little did I know, that walk into the emergency that night would be the last time I would ever walk on my own two feet.

I spent the remainder of the holiday season and more in the hospital. I passed out in I.C.U. and all my organs shut down. My body went into Disseminated Intravascular Coagulation (D.I.C.) brought on by a staph infection. My blood was infected somehow, someway. Blood flow to my hands and feet were compromised and my kidneys were shutting down. Doctors couldn't determine what the cause was and estimated that my chance of surviving would be about 20%. It was really tough on my husband, Jon, to see me in such an unstable and non-responsive state. He was forced to make all medical decisions for me. That was the beginning of a known battle for my life.

Seven days later I woke up. I was on a ventilator, I couldn't speak, I couldn't move. I realized I was very sick and I understood I was a dying girl. In the peace and quiet, I experienced a brief moment of sadness, at the thought of leaving my family behind, missing so much here on earth. However, being a woman of faith, and fully trusting in His will for me, my purpose and my family, I said a prayer. "Ok Lord, I know I'm yours and I know where I'm going, whatever Your will is," and I had complete peace and confidence that the Lord was with me. He promised! Joshua 1:9.

Many might ask, *"is this woman for real!? Did she really just accept that death was such an acceptable option, just like that!?"* To that I say "yes!" I've always found myself surrendering that prayer; it is a key objective living as a Christian. That's why Jesus died for us, to carry ALL our hurts, pains and sin. We as humans want to hang on to all the stuff, but when we learn to surrender to Jesus, we can have a peace that surpasses all understanding. With breast cancer, I realized I had to except my trials as a "friend."

"These things I have spoken to you, that in Me you may have peace. In the world you will have tribulation; but be of good cheer, I have overcome the world." John 16:33

Because of the lack of blood flow to my limbs, my hands and feet had open wounds which were wrapped up in bandages. I was unable to do anything for myself and it was very humbling to have total strangers giving me sponge baths, especially when it was a male nurse. My husband would read the Psalms to me. He showed me relaxing pictures of nature, the mountains, the ocean, lush green meadows; he knows me well. Doctors estimated I had about a month to live at best; D.I.C. means death is coming to doctors. In such critical condition, no visitors were allowed, they didn't even want me taking phone calls.

In order to increase my chances of survival and give my kidneys (which were functioning at less than 8%) the kick start they needed, I had to start dialysis. They had to take me off pain meds in order to try to wean me off the ventilator which meant that I got to experience an indescribable pain where my body lacked proper blood flow throughout my limbs. The doctors said "pain is good as it is part of the bodies healing process," but it was wearing.

By New Year's Day we clung to a little bit of good news. I was breathing on my own without the help of the ventilator and I was able to eat a little bit. My voice was coming back. The small victory lifted my spirit, it gave me some hope to cling to and a little strength to keep pushing. Doctors confirmed that I would, in fact, have to lose my finger tips on my right hand due to the damages from D.I.C. and my toes were likely going to go as well. My husband read to me all the prayers and well wishes that friends were sending our way. We knew the prayers were being answered. I was off the ventilator, eating meals and against all odds, I was still kicking. I wanted my husband to let everyone else know that "I'll be back." Knowing I was in good hands, I felt more peace than others around me could believe. Some might call it denial, but I call it faith. I assured my husband on several occasions, "Don't worry my love, I'm going to be okay..." *Even if I was in heaven I knew that was true.*

After about 20 days in the hospital, I was stable enough to have surgery. Doctors gathered around me trying to figure out whether they were going to amputate my hands above the wrist and my legs above my knees, but one Doctor out of six said, "wait! Mrs. Moore, do you mind waiting on amputations to see what we can salvage?"

I of course, said, "YES!" The only catch was that I didn't know how long I would have to wait, and amputating now would eliminate a lot of the pain right now. As my husband so eloquently stated in one of his email updates to friends and family, "I will not water the truth down and say we are doing great... The fact is this is very difficult and prolonged and many times Deborah and I struggle to keep our faith up as this seems never ending..." It was very trying for the both of us.

I spent 48 days in the hospital. I had a lot of time to think. I had so many questions swirling around in my mind. *How could this have happened? I was always eating healthy, exercising, clean and aware of germs, so where did I go wrong?* With all the time I had to ponder, question and cry, I'm thankful I never went to the "dark side". I think working in the medical field, I saw and heard about those who go into depression and it was as if a live person was dead. I once heard this, "to be in despair is to be without God", and this has stuck with me. I know God is always there for us, He is waiting for us to call Him. I would always call on Him. I realized how dark it could get, one morning, when they brought me breakfast and left it in front of me. I was alone. I looked at that plate full of food, thinking how am I going to eat? I felt like they were expecting me to eat, but they seemed to forget that my hands were wrapped up in bandages and, I couldn't grasp anything. I just started bawling and crying out to the Lord to help me not feel this way. I didn't want to feel so helpless, so dependent. I prayed and shared my pain with God. Five minutes later a nurse walked in and saw my situation and said, "Oh honey, I'll help you eat." I started bawling again, because she was so tender. She prayed over me and I was very comforted and His peace filled me.

Jon convinced the doctors to discharge me on the premise that if any signs of infection resurfaced I was to report back immediately. It felt so good to be home, even if it involved a hospital bed, bed pan, shower bench, transfer chair, antibiotics, medications galore, time sheets for medication, bandages up to our neck with ointments to last years. We had frequent doctor appointments. Our doctor visits were so regular, we felt we lived there. My husband joked with the doctors that "you should just put me on the payroll". I withstood excruciating pain in hopes to salvage my hands, legs and feet but the infection was compromising my chances of being able to live, let alone, "stay whole".

The months leading up to the surgeries were difficult and prolonged and many times I struggled to keep my faith up as it seemed never ending. However, one good thing about deciding to hold off on the surgeries, I was able to deal with the amputations psychologically. The limbs turned blacker and blacker and you could see where the healthy skin meets the dead skin. I now understood what the doctor meant by waiting to see what we could salvage. Watching my limbs turn black, I was able to face the fact that I couldn't use them, they were dead, we needed to get rid of them.

I was home for about a month before we returned to the hospital. The doctors explained to me how and when they would amputate. They would do one leg at a time below the knee, wait a couple days and amputate the next leg. A Physiologist came into my room the next day and now both legs below the knee had been amputated. He didn't even wait till Jon was there to support me. He woke me up from my sleep around five thirty in the morning and said, "Mrs. Moore your legs have been amputated. We will start therapy to help you learn how to get in and out of the bed, but you will never walk again." The bedside manner was terrible and insensitive and cold, then he left the room. I was so mad, mostly at how he handled telling me. Jon came in around eight o'clock that morning and I started bawling in his arms. I stayed in the hospital a couple more weeks, worked hard in my physical therapy, and then went home to heal.

The more time I spent at home, the better I felt, but it wasn't over yet. I returned back to the hospital after another couple weeks for surgery on my hands, one hand at a time. The hands take more time because of all the little vessels, nerves, veins, ligaments, tendons, skin and bones. When it was time to unwrap the bandages from my amputated hands, the first thing I said was, "my hands look so ugly," and I cried.

My aunt used to tell me "rub your hands with a dab of Vaseline and a few drops of lemon juice to keep my hands soft and pretty."

I did, and they were "the prettiest little hands," my husband would say as he kissed them. I would scratch his back and his neck with my long healthy trimmed finger nails. I accepted the knowledge of amputations, I had no choice. The start of a new journey, begins. Time to adjust to a new normal.

Jon was by my side the entire time. Through technology, he kept our friends and family up to date and let people know that we needed lots of prayer. He really stepped up to the plate, living up to his vow to care for me "in sickness and in health till death do us part." He made me his #1 priority and we put our faith in God for our finances to remain relatively intact while we could not work. I could not work for obvious reasons and he decided that caring for me took precedence above all else. I had no idea I was marrying such a wonderful, faithful caretaker. If he was going to take any work opportunity it was going to be a flexible one that worked around our schedule. In his email updates to friends and family he was so sweet as to announce, "I finally have a job I love" and, "Although I keep asking for a raise, she says no... And I have been written up a few times..." My personal favorite is "I know for some this will be hard to understand, but money is nothing compared to the one you love. Take care of the things God loves and he will take care of you."

We experienced refreshing moments of laughter when Jon would brush my hair and put it up, my ponytail often ended up lopsided. He even played cosmetologist and attempted to do my makeup. Needless to say my face resembled that of a clown... Blending isn't his forte. I have been reassured through this process that he is committed to me till the end. He has been my hands and feet nursing me to health. I am truly blessed and grateful for such a man who loves unconditionally. He prays for me and didn't want me to be a memory in his life and now he's stuck with me. I married a keeper.

A year into this journey, I had already undergone twenty surgeries, so we started to be more mindful of the decisions we were making with doctors' list of upcoming procedures on our agenda. We understood that they might not agree with our decision to decline or postpone certain procedures. But we needed a little break due to aftermath of surgeries. Sometimes you need to listen to your own body and we needed a break from lost independence, high pain levels and high risk with anesthesia.

The break helped very much and helped both of us focus on adapting to our situation.

Going through this whole experience at the beginning I felt like my whole world was taken. I felt like it was all a dream and I was going to wake up, but every time I tried to get out of bed or looked in the mirror and noticed my new handicap, I was reminded that this was real. I felt a never ending heartbreak and mourned the loss of my limbs. I felt like I was in a prison within myself, unable to do anything for myself, robbed of my independence. As my world stood still, I would sit by the front window looking out to see everyone kept living life as normal. Families were taking a walk, riding bikes, going to work, and smiling, while I was stuck in a chair doing nothing! It was unbearable. I wanted to jump out and run on my feet and drive my car. Dare I say, I even wished that I could wash dishes and clean my house. I never thought I would want to do that again.

It is amazing the everyday things we take for granted when we are in good health. I kind of laugh now because 10 years ago you would not have found me thinking "I wish I could vacuum and clean the toilets, do the dishes and wash the car". But there I was wishing, when I could only wait. I could pray and read the Bible. I was able to get out and about with the help of Jon and my Go Chair. I could smell the fresh air and hear the birds singing and see how beautiful God's creation is. I went on a date with my husband and while looking out at the ocean and shoreline where I once jumped, walked and swam, tears began to flow like a river. I was reminded how my feet felt walking in the water with the sand going through my toes and my feet sinking as each wave splashed upon me. These reminders of life the way it was, could happen anytime, anywhere.

Prosthetics is a whole different world. Wow! There are over a thousand types of prosthetics out there, each are engineered by someone who thinks they've found the perfect foot, leg, hand, or arm. There are some really good ones out there, but none can mimic the almighty design of our Creator. We had to wait for the wounds from surgeries to heal on my legs. We visited our first prosthetist (the specialist who fits you and whom we will refer to as Dr. P. moving forward). He measured around the residual limbs and created casts to make a mold where they are sent to be built. It was a time consuming process, going once a week for fittings, I started on a level one foot to learn balance. This was very tedious for me. Coming from a life full of physical activities, playing racquet ball, swimming, and jogging.   I just wanted the most energetic foot to get on my way. This was taking too long. I wanted to move! When I tried my set of legs, it was an exciting, tearful day of standing and taking my first baby steps. Dr. P. already knew I would become a walker by how well I was doing. She knew I wanted to walk. She said, "some people come in with one leg missing and they don't have the will to walk."

Being a bilateral amputee was even more difficult to fit. My first doctor didn't have any experience fitting a bilateral. Back and forth we went to get adjustments. I practiced walking in the hallway of my home with a special walker. Down the hallway like a toddler trying to keep balance. There was pain on my residual limbs from the pressure against the socket and that's why I would have to go back and forth for adjustments. It's a very complicated process.

After a week of practicing in my hallway, I was fed up, it was too painful and frustrating. I gave up! I sat down, cried and prayed, "Lord this hurts too bad, I can't do this, it's too hard. If I'm going to walk, You have to help me. I need You!" I went to bed and the next morning, when I felt more rested, I gave it another shot. I was standing in my kitchen and thought, "I wonder if I could take a few steps without the walker, my kitchen counters were close enough to lean on if I went down." I pushed the walker out of the way, leaned on the kitchen counter, let go and took my first steps without the walker! I was amazed! I called Jon, "Look! I just took my first steps without the walker!" Jon was amazed, we both laughed and cried with joy. It was the beginning of the new Deborah walk. A year later, it was still painful. Three different doctors couldn't get the fit right. We prayed, tried over and over to get a fit, we were patient with the doctor but I couldn't help but wonder, *am I ever going to be able to walk again without pain?*

One day I found another woman who lost her limbs. I wanted to meet her so we could talk about things in common. We emailed each other and I happened to ask her, "by the way, how do your legs fit?"

She said, "they fit great! I love them!"

I asked, "Where are you going for your prosthetics?"

"Southern California Prosthetics in Irvine, here is their number," she replied.

I called that day and was able to speak with the doctor himself. An appointment was made for the next day. It was a Godsend meeting, an answer to my prayers. My needs were met above and beyond. I met other amputees in the office and we talked and learned from each other. At the other place, I had no interactions with other amputees. Irvine was like a living room setting, full of lovely people. I still go there after six years and they have blessed me with amazing feet, a learning facility and great friends. Freedom Innovations gave me some feet to test and keep including swim feet and sent my husband and I to Florida for a Trade show all inclusive for a week. I learned so much and have been blessed beyond what I expected. I am very grateful for these companies and the people who have been such an integral part of my recovery.

This journey has directed me to become a stronger believer and more committed than I have ever imagined. Through all the prayer that our friends and family have lifted up, I have witnessed so many miracles in both my life and in the lives around me. I have become very humble through this experience. I wanted to kiss my children and make sure they were aware that I love them very much. Sometimes you think they know, but we have to say it, with a hug and kiss. I spend more quality time with Jon and he with me. We have great conversations and special moments of laughter. We are closer than ever and we love each other more and more. We don't take fevers lightly. Life is short and sometimes taken suddenly so we have learned to not fret over the small things. My knowledge of the living God, Jesus Christ my Lord and Savior, has been my Rock and my Fortress. Psalm 94:22. The Bible is my recipe for Life. It's God's love letter to us. I read the bible, fellowship and listen to the word, worship music and I pray always. I can't image having experienced this trial without my loving Savior, supportive husband, family and friends who also prayed, cooked, cleaned my house and encouraged me and cheered me on along the way.

Jon and I have had the opportunity to share our testimony and will continue to do so. We celebrated 31 years on our last anniversary and have been blessed with two perfect little grandsons. They have been a gift to this family and have added to the many joys that we have experienced in my recovery. The other day, my five year old grandson asked me, with his finger on his chin, "Grandma, where are your feet and fingers?"

I told him, "they are waiting for me in Heaven."

"Then, why is it taking so long?" He replied.

I took a deep breath and said, "Only God knows the time, when He's ready, but right now I have to stay busy sharing His love story."

With a huge smile he replied, "oh!!"

Today, after much physical therapy, patience, practice and encouragement, I can ride a bike. I can swim, drive my car, hold my grandsons and play soccer with them, plant in my garden, wash my dishes, clean my house, wash my clothes, paint, write with a pen, cook some meals and dance with my husband. I now have special swim feet. They are fins that attach to my prosthetics and I kind of feel like a mermaid in the water now.

One of my latest triumphs took place at the beach. I walked into the ocean, put my fins on and I was able to wet my gills once again! It was the most amazing experience swimming in the ocean once again, one of my favorite things to do. I swam like a freed fish. The water was cold, fresh and exhilarating! I kept swimming, free style to back stroke to free style and then it hit me like a brick wall. I flipped over to float on my back and cried out to the Lord to say, "Thank you!"

With tears flowing, I said to those who were around me, "We take our feet and our hands for granted! This is great! Thank you for swimming with me!"

I turned over and kept swimming and enjoyed the moment. We went back to shore after thirty minutes; it was cold, but worth every minute. The sun was shining and my family and friends shared the rest of the day at the beach. Later I convinced everyone who was there to take another swim with me. I could hear one of my cousins say,

"I feel young again! I haven't done this in years! Thank you Deborah!" I was blessed, we all cried joyful tears.

Revisiting that certainty about death I had in the hospital bed: Life here is short, but life in Christ is forever. I am no longer here for myself, but for the Lord. Each day is special and God can use you to touch someone in your day with a smile, helping hand, time to listen, to give. Each sunset is God's signature, God loves me and He loves you. I knew then and I know today, when I die, I will go to Heaven. It's a remarkable place, it shines like precious stones. We can only imagine how beautiful it will be. *Who wouldn't want to go there? Are you ready? Do you know where you're going when you die?* I am confident because,

> *"For God so loved the world that He gave His one and only Son, that whoever believes in Him shall not perish but have eternal life..." (John 3:16-21).*

We all have a choice to make in whatever life trials we may be going through and that choice is, we can walk into a dark cave or walk into the light that Jesus gives. Have faith that God will work a miracle out of this trial. Though evil and darkness overshadows us we know it will not have the victory... That is God's promise and we hold on to it. God is using this not only to bring people together in prayer but also to witness his power at work in our lives. You can't go wrong walking with The Great Physician! Have a beautiful life with your family and friends and cherish each and every moment!

Pick Yourself Up
And Dust Yourself Off

Aside from squishy little newborns who are kept in a bubble for as long as possible, I have yet to meet a person who has never experienced a trial in their life. What do we do when there is a trial or a set back? Do we give up? Do we seek help? Do we declare a state of panic and alert the media? There are so many different ways to conquer our trials. Life is like a dance. One step forward and two steps back. We all fall down. The most important thing you can do is pick yourself up, dust yourself off and keep moving forward in the direction that leads to where we need to be.

Confession time: I am a sucker for the Olympics and all the amazing athletes who compete. They have literally trained their whole life, blood, sweat and tears. My heart breaks when I see the athlete who falls in the middle of the race; but nothing moves me more than the moment when you see him pick himself up, dust himself off, and finish the race. The crowd goes wild and onlookers are all in tears. Why? Because they didn't give up! They had faith in themselves that they could and would finish. Even if they didn't get a spot on the podium, they still get to hold their head high knowing they did their very best. Deborah has faith in God to help her keep a positive perspective. Despite the seemingly impossible challenges she faced, her higher power gave her the strength to see the light. Christine uses her faith to give her the strength she needs to pick herself up, dust herself off and keep moving forward.

Christine Sanchez

As a child, I had dreams. I wanted to meet my prince charming, have children, and become a teacher. Typical little girl dreams. I never dreamed that my life would be hard, that I would have to fight battle after battle, that I would shed so many tears. The one thing that got me through it all was my faith.

In 2005, I came out of an abusive relationship and was starting a new chapter in my life. I felt like I was practically starting from scratch. I moved back in with my parents, got a new job, and enrolled myself back into college. I worked my butt off day and night, blood, sweat and tears. I was completely dedicated to my work and my education. My days consisted of work, school and church. There wasn't much time for anything else. In 2008, I graduated from college with an AA degree, and transferred to San Jose State University. I was both happy and proud that I was on my way to becoming a teacher. In February 2009, I met an amazing man who swept me off my feet and was everything I had prayed for and so much more. Things were finally coming together. I was the happiest I had ever been.

While doing homework one evening in November 2009, I rubbed my left eye and my heart sunk to my stomach when I discovered that I couldn't see out of my right eye. Initially, I thought maybe it was just my astigmatism getting worse and that eye glasses would fix the problem. The next day I made an appointment with our family eye doctor. First, the doctor tested my eyes by having me read the chart of letters. My left eye passed with flying colors, but my right eye completely failed. I couldn't see a single letter. Second, he shined a bright light into my eyes. The left eye was fine, but when he shined the light into my right eye the look on his face changed. He didn't say anything at first. He shined the bright light into my right eye a few more times, turned off the lights in the room and shined the light into my right eye again. He then told me that my right pupil was slow to dilate and constrict. He was not sure what was causing this and he advised me to make an appointment with my primary doctor. I was a little scared, a little worried, but I never thought it was serious. I had migraine headaches, but other than that, I was healthy.

I contacted my primary doctor who, in turn, referred me to an eye specialist. In February 2010, the eye specialist ran the same tests and confirmed everything the first eye doctor had found during his testing. The specialist was baffled and she had no clue what was going on. She then suggested an MRI to take a closer look at what might be causing this problem. I went from feeling a little scared and a little worried to full blown terrified and nervous.

On March 4th 2010, I got the phone call that changed my life... I had waited three long weeks for this call from my doctor regarding my MRI results. It was the longest three weeks of my life. She told me they found a tumor that had engulfed itself around my right optical nerve and two brain aneurysms. I calmly hung up the phone, walked over to my boss and told him I had to go home. He asked, "why?"

When the words "I have a brain tumor and two brain aneurysms" came out of my mouth, it became real. I wasn't dreaming. I emotionally broke down and sobbed uncontrollably.

I was devastated. My hopes, my dreams, it was all crumbling before my very eyes. All I had worked so hard for was coming to an end. I had to quit school so I could work fulltime, enabling me to be able to pay for the medical bills that were piling up. All I can remember thinking was, "why me?" *How could this happen? I am only 28 years old and I'm going to die. I don't want to die! I'm not ready to go yet!*

I had a team of specialists working on my case who all said this was a very complicated and they had never seen a case like mine before. *Very reassuring, right?! Not the best circumstance to be considered "special" in.* I was diagnosed with the rarest and most difficult type of aneurysm: a very large fusiform aneurysm. I was in and out of the hospital doing test after test, procedure after procedure, speaking to specialist after specialist.

I was then told that the tumor might be spreading to my pituitary gland and to my left eye. It was difficult to tell on the MRI, they saw spots and were concerned. I was absolutely petrified. They tested further and confirmed that the tumor was spreading to my pituitary gland and my left eye. They explained the spots were very small, the tumor seemed to be slow growing, and not to worry. *Yeah right, "don't worry."*

None of the neuro surgeons wanted to touch the aneurysms out of fear that I wouldn't survive the surgery. They gave me a 1 in 4 chance of surviving. My neuro oncologist suggested radiation treatment for the tumor. So in September 2010 I had radiation treatment. I remember laying there with tears rolling down my cheeks as they made my mask for the Cyber Knife Radiation treatment. They use this so that I remain still while the laser works its magic on my brain. I was scared. I had never gone through anything like this before. I couldn't believe this was happening to me. I endured five treatments; they decided only to treat the tumor engulfing my right optical nerve and leave my pituitary gland and left eye alone for the time being. The doctors were hopeful that this radiation treatment would keep the tumor from growing. I wasn't sure how to feel. They told me not to worry that they had the best of the best neurologists working my case and were meeting weekly to discuss my case. They sent me home and told me, "we will just have to keep a close eye on you."

The thought that I could possibly lose the vision of my left eye too, I can't even explain in words what I felt. The little things that I took for granted like cooking my own dinner, picking out my outfit for the day, doing my hair, doing my makeup, there was a chance that I may never be able to do these things again. Not only was there the possibility of me going completely blind, but I was living with a ticking time bomb in my head, quite literally. The word afraid doesn't even begin to explain what I felt. Knowing that the aneurysms could burst at any moment, that I could die at any moment was pure torture. There were days where the anxiety made it hard to breathe. It was overwhelming.

I prayed a whole lot through it all. I fell to my knees many times asking God "why?" I remember feeling so angry. I would curl up into a ball on the floor sobbing uncontrollably. I remember thinking "this is not fair". I had worked so hard. I have had to fight so many battles. I have had to overcome so much. I wasn't sure if I had it in me to fight this battle. After much prayer and many tears, it finally came to me. This wasn't my battle to fight. All I had to do was have faith. And that's what I did.

The man who came into my life in 2009, stayed by my side through it all. He didn't have to, we had only been dating for nine months when my health took this dramatic turn, but he chose to stay. He wiped many of my tears and he moved heaven and earth to make me smile. He was truly God sent. On June 2, 2012 he asked me to marry him. I was on top of the world again. One of my dreams would come true.

In 2013, while continuing to fight my brain tumor, they found a tumor in my left leg and also found that the large fusiform aneurysm had grown which meant something had to be done and had to be done quickly. I was crushed. I was in the middle of wedding planning. This was supposed to be the happiest time of my life, and at the same time I was writing out my wishes should I die. I remember asking the doctor if it was possible to push out my brain surgery for after my wedding so that at least one of my dreams would come true.

I had surgery on my left leg in July 28, 2013, got married September 14, 2013, had brain surgery October 24, 2013, and found out I was pregnant March 19, 2014.

The Lord is my Redeemer. God had a plan. While I did have to quit school to be able to pay for my medical bills, I was promoted four times at work. I married the man of my dreams and survived the brain surgery. God had a plan. Here I am, a year and half after my brain surgery happily married with a beautiful seven month old baby boy. My miracle baby. If that wasn't awesome enough, I am currently working with the Director of Humanities at San Jose State University to get back into school and fulfill my dream of being a teacher.

Currently, my condition is stable. During the brain surgery, the neuro surgeon was not able to remove the tumor due to its location. It would have caused more harm than good. The neuro surgeon was able to reinforce the walls of the large fusiform aneurysm to prevent it from rupturing in the future. Fusiform aneurysm are rare and hard to treat because they cannot be clipped off like most aneurysms. The neuro surgeon left the smaller aneurysm alone due to its size. While I still have the brain tumor, the good news is, it's stable and has not grown. The tumor spots on my pituitary gland and my left eye are stable and have not grown. Both aneurysms are stable and have not grown!! The doctors are hopeful and continue to monitor me closely. I have MRI's and angiograms done from time to time. I have my good days and my bad days. There are days where I realize I still have these things in my head. I start to think "what if these aneurysms burst? What if I go completely blind?" Then the Lord reminds me that he didn't bring me this far for nothing. I'm confident that I'm going to be okay. God has given me the strength to overcome. He has taught me to trust Him. I will continue to fight and continue to overcome until my last breath!

The journey has been rough, tough and bumpy, but the Lord never left my side. The Lord does not promise life is going to be easy. He promises to never leave us nor forsake us. He gave me a wonderful husband, wonderful family and friends to support me through it all these last five years. I've witnessed miracle after miracle. I feel God continuously shines his grace over me and my little family. I know there are more bumps ahead, but my faith is in the Lord and know he will protect me.

We all have a story. God gave each of us our own story. I believe the things that we go through in life are not meant to hurt us or break us, but to deepen our faith in the Lord, to strengthen us and most importantly to help others who are hurting.

Seasons

Like the weather, life has many different seasons. Some seasons are bright and sunny, others are gloomy and stormy. Sometimes the season lasts a few months and, depending on where you live, the season can last half a year. Life's seasons can even go on for years. But we all know that when we weather the storm, the brighter days come. The clouds clear even if just for a moment and the sun shines its light on the earth. More often we recognize the seasons with dark storms; we have no idea where they came from and it seems like no light is ever going to appear and we lose hope. While we are experiencing personal devastating hurricanes, we can't help but notice the person across the way basking in the sun with all that life has to offer, longing to join them. But there are experiences to be had and lessons to be learned and so it goes. Spring turns to summer and summer turns to fall and while our personal seasons can last much longer, every season has its end and when one season ends a new one begins and at least there is hope in that.

In my first book I shared the glass elevator analogy. I was trying to leave the bottom floor and move up to the next floor when the elevator stopped in between floors. I wrote about looking at the surroundings from that perspective, seeing if there was unfinished business on the first floor, or maybe taking a look at the second floor to map out what I wanted to do once I got there. What I neglected to write about was how frustrating it is to be in the same place or in that situation unwillingly. I so desperately wanted to move. I wanted to get to the next chapter of my life. I wanted that elevator to move and it wouldn't budge. I pushed buttons, I jumped up and down, I threw tantrums, I pressed my face against the window seeing everyone who was one level above and one level below me and cried out for help. After more time than I thought reasonable being stuck in the elevator I almost lost hope. I fell to the floor and cried as I was stuck in this uncomfortable place, because I felt I would be stuck there forever. Nothing I tried could make that elevator move. I was hopelessly waiting, until one day the power came back on and it moved.

Sometimes in life we feel that the current season will last forever and that the situation is the way the rest of our life will be. We see only the problem with no solution and project that this is how things will continue... forever... It seems there is no end in sight for our feeling of loneliness, isolation and despair. We believe the empty void we are struggling to fill will remain empty forever. In the midst of our struggle we believe that it will continue forever, forgetting that these are just seasons and that seasons change.

Remember, in these seasons, to have faith in the upcoming sunshine. Weather the storm with hope and faith and the sun will shine again. Your current situation is not a reflection of the rest of your life. Be patient. Understand that seasons change. Please remember that no matter what you are going through, no matter how dark the storm or how long it has been raining, a day will come where the sun will peak behind the clouds, revealing brilliant rays, and if you look hard enough you might just find the rainbow.

Deborah had a season of loss, where she continually lost parts of her own body. Amy had a season of heart ache. When their seasons of trail ended, they both experienced seasons of joy. This next author had a season of trials. She learned that there is "no growth in the comfort zone and no comfort in the growth zone." The rain for her may have been a little uncomfortable but she knew her rainbow was coming and, like a flower, she knew it would help her grow.

Saundra Ganem

Through series of fortunate and unfortunate events I have learned that there is no growth in the comfort zone and there is no comfort in the growth zone. When I left my comfortable suburban life in Philadelphia to achieve my dreams in Los Angeles, I learned just how uncomfortable that growth zone was.

Growing up I had a very blessed life. I came from a very supportive family with a mother and father and two older siblings.

It was like the perfect family you see in the movies. I attended a very reputable high school, played sports and after graduation attended a well-known college. I was also fortunate to have staffing agencies find me well paying jobs. Life was happy and went smoothly. To add the cherry on top of my blessed life I got the opportunity to move from my parent's house to sunny Orange County, California. I went to seek full time work to help pay my student loans off; but more importantly I was going to experience life in a new different and exciting place.

In 2012, I packed my bags with a one way ticket and headed to this beautiful new location. I went from my comfortable parent's house to my comfortable sister's house. So far so good. When I got to Orange County, I started looking for work and going to the gym. In fact, I was at the gym so much they gave me a job there. I had applied for the front desk greeter position. I figured my bubbly personally was great at welcoming people; however, the manager had another position in mind for me. She said I would make a great membership specialist. I had never done anything like that and it was a little out of my comfort zone, but I choose to take the challenge in the new position. I am not afraid of making mistakes and figured this was a great learning opportunity. While I was working at the gym I was still looking for a full time job as an administrative assistant. The economy at that time was really bad and I wasn't having any luck in the current job market. I wasn't enjoying sales and I wasn't making enough money to live on my own. After five months of living in California I decided I didn't like what it had to offer me, so I re-packed my bags, bought a plane ticket and flew back to my comfort zone, aka my parents house.

Once I was back in my comfort zone life went back to easy street. I landed a corporate full time job on salary. I didn't have to pay rent at my parents so saving money was easy. I fell into a routine. During the week it was work then Crossfit. On the weekends it was fun and Crossfit. I had everything that I could ever want. Life was great, but I wasn't happy. I couldn't figure out why I wasn't happy; I had everything I wanted and my life was set. *What could possibly be missing?*

My very good friend made me realize why I was struggling with truly being happy. He made me realize what I was subconsciously avoiding. I didn't know who I was. I was involved in what everyone else was doing. I was complacent in life; I was unaware that my life was just a mere passing of days. I wasn't pursuing what I truly wanted, which I still only had a little idea of what that even was. This realization was my breaking point. I felt stuck. Living complacent and living fulfilled are two completely different things. *Maybe the happiness I was looking for was on the other side of my comfort zone?* Getting out of my comfort zone was something I was familiar with. I liked the challenge. One example is when I was younger I wanted to play hockey. I didn't know how to skate but I accepted the challenge and learned. I have had a lot of experiences getting out of my comfort zone, but why was this time different?

An opportunity came again for me to move to California. One of my friends from high school was moving to Los Angeles and suggested I get a room in the same complex she was moving to. She gave me the contact information to the women I would be living with and I called her. She told me all about the room I would be occupying, it was already furnished, rent was on a monthly basis, no contract and it would be ready in a month. It was too perfect to pass up so I was set to move back out to California. The door that I thought might never open again just flew open and I had no doubt that I had to take this opportunity. Round two was about to begin.

I bought another one way ticket, packed a bag and headed back to California anxiously awaiting the unknown. After a long flight I was greeted by my sister and her family holding a neon pink sign saying, "Welcome to California Saundra!" I was so excited to be back. My sister drove me to my new house where I was welcomed by my high school friend and met my new roommate. We went out to dinner that night with a few of her friends. The food and the culture were a couple of the things I was looking forward to most. We danced all night at the local bars and I thought to myself life was going to be pretty fun in Southern California.

The next day my sister picked me up to go spend the weekend with her and her family in Huntington Beach. I had planned on just having fun that weekend and would start my job search on Monday. In Pennsylvania, my experience with temp agencies had always kept me working so I wasn't too worried about finding a job here. That weekend I reconnected with my friend Garrett who was a member of the gym I worked at during my first attempt at California life. When I had moved back he and I kept in contact and I am glad I did because he would become really important to my story.

As planned, when Monday rolled around, I started searching for jobs. I was still at my sister's awaiting my car to complete its journey to California. I spent half the day looking for jobs and the other half playing with my niece and nephew. I was receiving return calls for jobs and going on interviews so I felt things were going smoothly. Along with finding work, it was important to me to find a great Crossfit gym where I could meet a core group of friends. Between interviews I would check out gyms, but nothing felt like my home gym. One day I had gotten a call from a staffing agency in Century City which is a little metropolis outside of Los Angeles. I was excited! It was the land of opportunity and I just landed mine.

Let me tell you about just getting to the interview. There is this phenomenon in California called "traffic". I had avoided driving into Philly because of all the traffic and now I was driving in more hectic traffic without hesitation. Not only was the traffic overwhelming, I had made so many wrong turns trying to figure out the city, but I made it and on time! The drive took as long as the interview process did, about two hours. The interview consisted of telling my story to three recruiters and making a one minute video on why companies should hire me. I was exhausted by the end of the whole process, but I felt I did really good and was optimistic while I tried to figure out how to get out of the parking garage with no money on hand.

Soon after the interview, the agency called me with a potential job. This job was in a sky scrapper in downtown LA. I had never worked in a city setting and this seemed appealing to me. I told them "absolutely" and submitted my resume for the job. I was excited I had a potential job in the big city and I was really hopeful this was the break I needed. A few weeks went by and I hadn't heard anything from the company. I decided to be proactive and give them a call, only to find out they had chosen someone else for the position. I was bummed about this opportunity falling through but was hopeful that something better must be coming. I had some money in savings and felt secure at the moment but at night when, worry was most apparent, I questioned if I had made the right choice by coming back to California. *Would I ever find a job that would pay well enough for me to live here and continue my education?* My thoughts would creep back to my first attempt at California living and the failure that I experienced; but this time felt different. This time I had a better chance and this time I was going to make it. I just needed to be patient and not settle for the first opportunity out of convenience. This time it will work out. I was here for a reason and I wasn't going to throw in the towel just yet.

The day before Thanksgiving I was walking on the pier of Redondo Beach. I was getting ready to meet with my parents, who had flown into town for the holidays, when I received a call from the staffing agency. They told me the person they had hired for the skyscraper job wasn't a good fit and they would like to offer the position to me, but they wanted to meet with me that day. My interview was at 5:00 pm and as I made it up to the 36th floor of the sky scrapper, my first view was of the sunset hitting the Hollywood sign. I had never seen anything so beautiful and knew in my heart this is where I wanted to be. The interview went smoothly. All of the practice I had with interviews the few weeks prior had prepared me for this moment. At the end of the interview they offered me the job; I was to start on Monday with the title of Executive Assistant. You can say I had a lot to be thankful for that Thanksgiving! My family was in town at my sister's house, I had my health, a great new job and I was living in Southern California.

The start of my job came and went. Saying I underestimated the traffic would be an understatement itself. I had never seen anything like this, but figured, like most new experiences, it would just be something I would have to get used to. I would leave my house at 5:45 am and get to work by 7:30 am. My days were long as I would leave work to go to Crossfit, sit in traffic and hour and a half then leave Crossfit to sit in traffic another hour to get home. I was young and had no one but myself to worry about so it was ok for me. Some people called me crazy and some called me dedicated. I called myself both!

Crazy me continued this routine for a few months. I enjoyed my job and although it was only a temp job I was told if I did well they would hire me full time. Every day at work I busted my butt and did the job to my best ability. I wanted that job and I was going to prove I deserved it. My job had a two week holiday so I flew back home to spend that time with my family. Upon my arrival back to California my luggage had gone missing. The airline informed me they would have it to me later that week. I didn't have a lot of clothes and this was a huge inconvenience for me. Trying to stay positive, I was thankful I had the essentials like my wallet and my glasses. While at work on Wednesday I received a call from my mom. She called to ask why my bank account was negative $900. I had no idea because I was good with balancing my money and knew there had to be a mistake. I called the bank and they advised that I was a victim of fraud. They didn't know how this had happened, but they were investigating and they would return the money as soon as they figured out the problem. I had just given my roommate the rent check and had called her to tell her about the fraud and to not cash the check. I knew things like this happened and I knew I would have to deal with stuff like this sooner or later. Although I had no luggage, and no money I tried to not let this affect my work or my positive attitude.

By the week's end, both my luggage and my money had been returned just in time for my mini vacation I had planned with friends. We spent the weekend in the beautiful Park City, Utah. We had a lot of fun and enjoyed the beautiful surroundings. When I had gotten back from my mini vacation my roommate came into my room and told me we needed to talk. She had explained that my rent being late was unacceptable and I needed to leave. She gave me two options; if I left the next day I could have my rent back or I had to be out by month's end. I was devastated and upset that she was so harsh and didn't take the fraud into consideration. I called my mom for some comfort and direction. I had felt so alone and fearful of what to do. The next day I contacted everyone I knew on a lead for a new place to live. I didn't want to move, but figured this was an opportunity to move closer to work and shave a little of that drive time off.

Back to the home search, I reached out to Garrett and asked if he had any leads on a place to live in Los Angeles. He told me he would ask his friends but he himself was actually looking for a roommate in Huntington Beach. That was even further from my job, back in Orange County. That wasn't my plan, but I needed a place to live, so I told him I would consider it. A few days later,

Garrett convinced me to go look at the condo after work. He told me once I saw it I would fall in love with it. I took the drive from LA to HB in rush hour traffic and he was right: I did fall in love with the place. The people who owned the condo told me they had given Garrett till that day to find a roommate and if he didn't they were going to go with another interested couple. They also said they were looking to have it filled at the exact same time that I needed to be out of my current place. Talk about timing! It's incredible the way things work out. I have come to learn timing is everything, nothing is an accident, and things happen RIGHT ON TIME. The commute was going to be a little uncomfortable for me, but it was beautiful and the timing was right, so I said, "Yes."

After a month of living in HB I was settled in and found my new routine of work and Crossfit. A few extra miles of driving and a little more time in traffic wasn't too much to deal with. I loved my job and I knew any day it would become my permanent job. This was just something I would have to get used to. I was busting my butt at work and getting along well with everyone. Every Friday, I ordered breakfast for the whole office. There were usually leftovers and felt we should take that food to a shelter. One particular Friday, there were extra bagels, muffins and pastries so I looked up a shelter to take them to. I found a children's shelter in Hollywood and donated the food there. While I was there I received a phone call from my staffing agency. I had hoped they were going to tell me I was getting permanently hired and I was smiling through the phone; I could tell something was off. She confirmed that, by telling me the company I was working for decided not to move forward with me. *How could this happen??* I proved myself over and over every single day there, going above and beyond what my job entailed. It was also a plus that everyone told me they liked me. I was puzzled and I felt led on. For three straight months, my boss kept telling me to keep doing a great job and I was going to be permanent. But clearly this wasn't the case. Again, I felt the familiar feeling of shock and discouragement. Those uncomfortable feelings were continuing to be a theme throughout my California experience. *Was California really for me?* With all the misfortunes that California had to offer me the four months, I wanted to run back to my comfortable Pennsylvania home. I had to break the news to my biggest supporter and encourager, my roommate.

While he was enjoying his vacation in Australia I had to break the news to him via FaceTime. I thought he would be mad or upset, but he calmly told me to keep moving forward and said three words that made me rethink giving up my California dream: " Adversity builds character." It's the truth. Hard times are going to show me what I'm made of. I can either choose to give up, or get through the times of struggle willing to accept whatever lesson it has to offer. I decided not to give up and run away; I had already learned so much about myself and other people out on my own, there was no way I could give up now. My friend John from

Crossfit Royalty told me before I moved that I should be a motivational speaker and write a book. I kept thinking about how many times my friend Bill told me I was an inspiration, helping him move forward and continue doing what is best for him. They were small reminders that I was in California for a reason. Moving home would not do anything for all the progress that I had already made.

My new job search offered me the opportunity to search for a job closer to home. Like my apartment situation, my job fell apart so something even better could come together, though I couldn't see what that was, it was a true blessing in disguise. The experiences I was looking for in LA fell apart so my life could come together in HB. The temp agency I had worked for in Los Angeles was affiliate with a temp agency in Orange County so they referred me and they started finding me work right away. They called me with a great opportunity that started the following week. Though it was a temporary position, and the pay was not as great, it was much closer to my condo and had potential for a permanent position. That's the thing about working through staffing agencies; I had to be flexible, positive and have faith that something would work out. I was going to continue with my hard work ethic and faith, prepared and aware it might happen or it might not.

I really liked the environment of this job and I started getting to know the assistants. Kiki and I started hanging out, she invited me out one Friday night with her boyfriend and their friends. Kiki and her boyfriend, Adam were so friendly and welcoming, I felt comfortable with them right away. I packed a bag, made my way there Friday and I ended up staying the entire weekend at their apartment. Besides my roommate, they were the first group of people with which I felt a true connection. They were not just a couple of people my age to hang out with, they were also friends I could confide in and by the end of the weekend, I felt they knew who I was as a person and I knew their hearts as well.

Along with Kiki making me feel welcome, I knew this job was for me when one of my bosses bought a pull up bar for work. As I was doing pull ups at lunch with Kiki one day, one of my coworkers came into the room and asked if I did Crossfit. He could tell right away that I did. I told him I was going to one in Huntington Beach and he mentioned he is a part-time coach at Crossfit in Newport Beach. He told me he was coaching that night and to come by after work. I was so nervous, but I had my gym bag packed and I would be disappointed in myself if I didn't try it out so I told him I'd be there.

Crossfit Newport Beach has been home away from home. I felt comfortable the first day I went. It reminds me of Crossfit Royalty back home. I have made some amazing friends there and that's what I was hoping for. There's something about Crossfit that truly connects you with other people who also Crossfit. We know we are crazy, but we have that bond. You struggle and suffer together through the same work out, but simultaneously enjoy the challenge and difficulty of it. Then you bond over it at the end and talk about it. I carry a lot of the lessons I've learned at Crossfit into all other aspects of my life; every day is a challenge. You're going to have ups and downs, good days and bad days and inconsistencies no matter how much experience you have, but how do you get through those challenges and progress?

This journey to California has not been an easy one, but I often wonder where I would be if I had stayed in my comfort zone. What would have happened if I didn't take the risk and follow my heart? I started this journey looking for the piece of me that I felt was missing in my life. Turns out the piece that was missing wasn't missing at all. It was just waiting to be awakened within me, to be set free. It was me needing to live, to experience life, my soul looking for its wings. If I could give you one piece of advice to live your life, it's my main mantra: There is no comfort in the growth zone and no growth in the comfort zone. I encourage you (and myself) to jump out of your comfort zone, take that risk! Whether it is a big thing like moving across the country or small thing like eating at a new restaurant with exotic food, whether it is a good result or bad result, you WILL learn from it. I have been living in California for six months now. I continue to learn about myself and other people and I am excited to continue to create the best version of myself. Humans are curious creatures, creatures of movement. We were made to explore all that life has to offer and have faith over fear. I am continuing my adventure in Southern California. There's a certain amount of vulnerability and fear that surfaces on a daily basis but I've learned in a short period of time that I'll be okay. I am learning that when challenges arise, I can toast to the opportunity that the future holds because the opportunities are endless. The more I learn of life's experiences, the more I feel complete.

Part II: Self Love

It's the good ol' Disney fairy tale; you are born, grow up, find your significant other, fall in love and live happily ever after. From a very young age we are taught that the reason we live happily ever after is because we have our significant other and we are in love. In most of the movies the girl's life is sad or challenging and when she meets her prince, the world gets better. Cinderella, for instance, is bossed around by her family, spends times with her animals and just dreams of a better life. Then she meets her prince, he sweeps her off her feet and they live happily ever after. I loved Disney movies growing up, but the message of these movies and of society is that we will find happiness inside relationships or that in order to live happily ever after, we must find our significant other. I would love to see past the credits where Cinderella realizes she has abandonment issues from her dad dying and she has trust issues for the way her step mom treated her. I would love to see past the honeymoon stage where they realize happiness isn't from the other person and if they are looking for it there they will not be happy for long. You see, although the world has placed such weight on finding happiness from our relationships, they forget to mention the most important relationship you will ever have is with yourself.

There is one person you have to live with from the time you are born to the very second you die and that person is you. It would be a very long miserable life if you had to spend all that time with someone you didn't like. On the other hand it could be a fun, magical life if you can spend it with a person you love. Isn't that the goal? Find a person you love and spend the rest of your life with them? It is important to find that person in yourself first. If you are looking for love from others you will be disappointed that they are unable to fill that love you are looking for. Love starts from the inside and then can be given outside. If you have no light can the room be lit? If you have a candle and carried it with you, would everywhere you go then have a light? Too often we are looking for love, or looking for someone to complete us, when we were born whole to begin with. On our journey to find love we must fall in love with ourselves first. Part two of the book is about the relationship we have with ourselves. Although we share about the relationship we had with others we learned valuable lessons and in turn learned to love ourselves first. If you are single, in a relationship or married we hope these next stories will inspire you and if nothing more help you grow in love and in understanding.

Compassion
Judgment Free Zone

There is a saying that before you can judge someone, you need to walk a mile in their shoes. Even after you have walked a mile in their shoes I feel you still don't have a right to judge because you didn't walk the mile before that with them, or any of the hundreds of miles they walked before that. You may walk along side them for a while and get a feel for their position but unless you are them you will never understand. As humans we have a tendency to make a judgment call based only on our perspective of what we feel is right for us. We see someone doing something we wouldn't and think negatively about that person or that situation, but what would happen if we came to people with a heart of compassion, or came to them with love? What would happen if we made an attempt to meet them where they are at in a judgment free zone and come with a heart of understanding? Where as a society would we be?

There are times in life where we see another person and we think "what are they doing with their lives?" We look at them and think, well if they would just do A, B, C they would be happier or they would do "better". Those thoughts are very common but A,B,C might not work for that person, or better yet A, and C, are things they really don't want in their lives. Meaning, the standards we created for our lives are not the standards that everyone on this planet should be held to. A child growing up thinks the way they experience life is the way everyone experiences life. If they get spanked for talking back, they think everyone else gets spanked for that. Somewhere along the line when children are about 10-ish they realize that there are different ways to live. Some families have a mom and a dad, some just have a mom. They realize that not everyone has the same situations. If a child can realize this, how, as adults, do we lose that innocence and harden our hearts to only see the "right way of living" through a tiny perspective of what we deem is right?

It is fair to say that everyone on this planet has had very different experiences in life. We talked earlier about how two people can be in the same situation but, through perspective, experience the situation very differently. Each person learns or doesn't learn differently from their experiences and they will make their choices in life based on that . Let's revisit the two people in traffic. The next morning one guy decides he is going to get up a little earlier and give himself more time to get to work. The other person decided he was going to take side streets and avoid the free way all together. Both made very different decisions, one might have made the decision you would have made, but that doesn't make the other person wrong for the choice they made. They both made a decision based on what works best for them.

Having a heart of compassion means not judging someone for making a choice you wouldn't make yourself. It means allowing people to live a life that best fits them. We don't know why a person is making a choice to do things the way they are. A while ago I was fired from my full time job. Everyone I knew asked the question, "what are you going to do now? Where are you going to work?" I made a choice that worked best for me and my life. I chose to not look for a job but to really focus on building my company, Stay Safe. Jim Carry said in a speech, "You can fail at what you don't want, so you might as well take a chance on doing what you love." I decided to take a chance at doing what I love because I had already failed at what I didn't want.

At that moment I really got to see people's true colors. My parents reacted with a heart of love and worry. What if it doesn't work and you go broke? You need money to live and you need to eat and they verbalized all the concerns parents would have. Understandable, but with love they also accepted it was my life and gave me the compassion or grace to try. Another person in my life judged me harshly and thought I was the worst person on the planet. In their eyes I was going to end up homeless, starving and "sucking off the planet's resources." For this person, simply trying wasn't good enough and wasn't something they would personally do. Being a respectable member of society you must work X amount of hours in a "real job." For one person I was living my life, and the other I was ruining my life and somehow theirs. Regardless of anyone else's perspective, I had to make the decision that best fit my life.

A few years back, a friend of mine had taken their own life, leaving behind her three month old baby. I began to think how selfish and how stupid they were and I could never understand how anyone could be so selfish or so down that they would take their own life. I wept for that baby who would never know his mother and for the newly widowed father who was left to raise his son alone. My friend Tiffany had the four smartest words that put everything into perspective for me. She said "be glad you can't." *Be glad I can't understand being so low that I take my own life. Be glad I don't understand.* I hear people all the time say I don't understand how a girl would stay with a guy like that, *be glad you can't.* I hear, I just don't understand how a person can live like that, *be thankful you can't understand.* Until you have walked a mile in that situation yourself to understand how it feels, you will never understand, and be glad you can't. When you look at someone's life and you don't understand how they got to where they are, meet them with love and compassion or meet them on a feelings level. At some point everyone has experienced a range of feelings; sadness, joy, pain, love, or loss to name a few. You don't have to understand a person's situation to understand the emotion they are experiencing. When you meet someone where they are with an open heart and without judgment, you can be helpful to them.

I never once understood how a girl could stay in an abusive relationship until I experienced firsthand how it can happen. I want to share my personal story here and I hope you can read it with an open heart. I could never understand... Until I could...

Jenae Noonan

"And I would like to welcome Jenae Noonan to Team USA. "These words brought pure joy and affirmation to my soul. My dream of competing on a world stage had just been fortified and with those words I was heading to the world games to represent the United States. With my mind focused on a gold medal, the words "when you least expect it, it will happen," proved true. I fell in love. It is funny how I can still remember the day, July 12th,

2012. It was a hot summer day in California where you can smell the asphalt itself melting away. I was still dressed in my training clothes as I walked in to the bike shop hoping to get a bike I could train on; instead, I left with my heart fluttering and smitten. I had met a handsome young man with dark hair and a mystery in his eyes that I was drawn to figure out. I had tickets to my favorite concert that same night and I asked him if he would like to go with me and that was the moment of no looking back. He said, "Yes".

I wanted to be with him every moment because he was funny, energetic, positive, sociable, and just loved life. He had an energy that drew me in and left me wanting more. I wanted to train and then run home to his arms. I spent hours at his shop while he worked just to be near him. Every moment of everyday I wanted to be near him. Literally only two weeks after we met I went on my family vacation and I couldn't bear to not have him with me so he came along. There could be a whole book on the importance of taking things slow but I threw all caution into the wind and fell in "love". He was it. He was the guy I was going to spend the rest of my life with. He was a charmer. He swept me off my feet, had my parents fall in love with him and had my mom planning a wedding. Well she does that type of thing all the time anyways, but at least now she could put a name to the groom in her plans. When we got back from our family vacation we made it Facebook official and became a couple. I couldn't have been happier. I finally had all my dreams in my hands. I had my dream of being a champion, my dream of owning a house, my dream car and finally, what had seemed to be my unicorn, I had my dream man. Life was great!

Here's the problem with falling so fast and so soon. You fall in love with an idea of love and know little about the person you "love." A week after we got home from the vacation, he cheated on me. The idea I had of love didn't include being cheated on, but I loved loving him and after he swore he would never do it again, I took him back into my happy little fantasy. *My first relationship boundary broken would only be the start.* As I was preparing for the world games my ideal of happy relationship was to have him with me at the games. After all, I loved him and wanted to share this moment with him. I worked hard to raise money to pay all the expenses for him to go with me. The day before leaving for the games, just three months into our relationship, he had gotten drunk and gave me an example of what I know now the rest of our relationship would look like. He called me every name under the sun, tore me down, and told me how much he really didn't like anything about me. At that point I was so "in love" and leaving for the world games the next day. I didn't have the courage to stand up for myself and show him that I wouldn't accept that type of behavior in my life. I forgave him as he promised to never do that again and I accepted the apology with open arms and left on a jet plane, with him. *Second relationship boundary destroyed.*

Once the behavior is accepted, it continues to get worse. Slowly he started to drink more and slowly the verbal assaults became daily. After a while he didn't need the alcohol to tell me what he thought of me. A once strong women became a robot. I became vigilant, watching what I wore so I didn't have to hear how he hated black, watching what I did when I got off work so I wouldn't be accused of cheating, cleaning as often as I could so I didn't have to hear how much of a lazy horrible human being I was. Instead of living my life and my dreams, I started withdrawing from society as I started to believe his words of my worthlessness. Every day I would go home and just be sick anticipating what I was going to hear. I remember sitting on the couch one night cringing as I heard him walking up the stairs. He opened his mouth to start yelling at me, for God knows what, and I remember asking him if we could have one night of peace; one night where I didn't have to hear anything. In his fashion, he told me if I didn't want to hear anything, maybe I shouldn't have been such a lazy b*tch and I should have cleaned the house that day. Without saying a word, I stood up, walked away locked myself in the bathroom and sat in the bathtub, with no water, because that was the only place that I could have some peace.

At first I would fight back. He would tell me how negatively he felt about me and I would try to defend myself. After a while I would just say, "Yep you are right I am ugly," not believing it at all but I just didn't want to argue. I just didn't have the strength anymore or I finally understood that it was not rational and there was just no point. If I changed because he didn't like black, the new blue shirt would be too low cut. If I spent all day cleaning the kitchen, why was the living room a mess? I remember the electricity getting turned off and if any of his fish died because it was off it would somehow, be all my fault. There really was no point in doing anything, or changing anything and I was learning to just take the verbal abuse instead of defending myself because maybe he would shut up sooner. I had just become a sheep, which ran at the site of the dog and cowered at the bark.

Then, there was *the* fight. I had become so broken that I rationalized to myself, *at least he never put his hands on me.* That was the last boundary that had not yet been crossed. I remember the night of his cousin's wedding. It was a lovely night and such a beautiful occasion. Everyone around was so happy, he and I knew to fake the happy well and we were the second, next to the bride and groom, happiest couple there. Truth was when I walked in and saw it was an open bar I was crying inside because there was only one way this night was going to end and it wasn't going to be pretty for me. After the wedding reception my highly intoxicated boyfriend was looking for anyone to look at him the wrong way. I begged him to get into the car so we can leave but a groomsman had to say something along the lines of "better listen to your girlfriend" and that's all it took. The glass mug that was in his hands flew across the street hitting the groomsmen's girlfriend and all hell broke out. Three or four guys started pounding on my boyfriend, which every ounce of me felt was well deserved. His sister, on the other hand, tried to get involved which got all the bridesmaids involved. Now there were three girls beating up my boyfriend's sister, three guys beating up my boyfriend and a bride screaming at me to "do something!" He may have never himself put his hands on me but putting me in a situation where I had to fight for his sister's safety and take on then two guys to help my now unconscious boyfriend, he might as well have put his hands on me. As I was driving off with my badly beaten boyfriend and his bloody sister, he went off on me telling me how stupid I was to make him look so stupid by defending him. We had driven about 5 miles from the party when he jumped out of my moving car to run back to the party to "show the guys he didn't need his girlfriend to defend him." At that point I was so mentally, emotionally and physically exhausted from the night, I drove off, leaving him on the side of the road.

That night as I drove home I had started thinking about my exit strategy. I could not live another day like this. I couldn't imagine living a life where every day I woke up and I just wanted to go back to sleep. I wanted a man to love me, but on a daily basis he listed all the reasons he hated me; a breath later told me he loved me but I knew in my heart that this wasn't love. This wasn't what I wanted for my life. There had to be someone out there who could at least like me more than he "loved" me. The fairy tale had ended and even if I spent the rest of my life alone I knew it couldn't be any worse than this. He had threatened to kill himself that night as he stood where I left him and my response was "tell me where so I can tell the coroner where to pick your body up", (this wasn't the first time he threatened to kill himself and at this point I was over that game too). His sister convinced me that it was best to at least try and find him. We spent rest of the night looking for him and at 7am he called his sister and gave us the location for his pick-up. No one talked on that hour drive home. A mentor of his talked to him about his behavior and he came home that night, with a look on his face that he understood how serious his actions were. Like a good manipulator he was, or how much of a sucker for a happy ending I was, I believed his "honest apology" and gave the relationship another try....again.

It only took a week, before I realized how insincere and fake his apology was and he was back to yelling and screaming at me. The night of the wedding, I saw a look in his eyes like the devil himself had possessed him and it was a look that scared me to my core. That day in my room I saw the look in his eyes as he began to throw things at me; I felt my life being threatened. When he could hear the sound of police sirens approaching the house he made a run for it and by the time they arrived, they found me, completely broken, scared and crying in fetal position on the floor. Finally I had had enough. The police informed me that if I were to press charges I might be me spending the night in jail because his mom was the witness and of course she would say I started it. Another reason I didn't press charges was because I was scared that him going to jail would hurt his feelings. I had just feared for my life, and yet I was still worried he might get hurt going to jail... The police said I had a few minutes to gather my most valuable things because I was going to go to a safe house.

It's a funny thing (if I can find any humor in what happened) the things you grab when you are told to grab what's important to you. The first thing I thought of was how horrible he was and the things he would do to hurt me so I grabbed the things I knew he would destroy. I have a collection of shot glasses from my adventures around the world and my parents gave as gifts from their travels. Those would be prime target for his rage so I grabbed those. I took my photo albums, picture frames, and my animals. I was then instructed that it might be a good idea to get credit card statements, and things that had personal information on it. I didn't know how long I would be gone but in my broken and scared mind my decisions were based on predicting how he would react. I grabbed a bag full of a few clothes and overnight items and left the house never to spend another night there again.

After that day I had no contact with him. He and his family were living in my house. My mom and her realtor friend continued to communicate with him as he made plans to move out. I sat at the house I was staying, in complete disbelief at where my life had ended up. *How does this happen to someone? How does someone allow this to happen to them? How did it get so bad? Why did I stay so long?* I literally couldn't look at myself in the mirror as I felt the guilt and the shame for where my life was. I had to make sense of it all and I decided I was going to write my story. I wrote my story in an article that was featured on a website. I shared it with the hope that I could help anyone who was going through the same love story. Maybe if my story helped someone I could make some sense of where I was at.

It took a very long time to pick up the pieces. When he had moved out I was allowed back on the property to collect a few more items and stage the house to sell it. I could never live there again for the fear he might come back, or know where I was and at this point. I owed my parents so much money, I had to sell it to pay them back. When I got there I was scared to see how he left the house or what he would have stolen. Even before I got in the door I noticed that he dug up and stole my pond along with all my Koi fish. I tried thinking, *what kind of person digs up a pond and steals it?* Then I remembered why I took my shot glasses. To be honest along with some other things he took, the theft of the pond was the hardest to get over. How much he hated me, how much work he put into trying to hurt me! Yes I was hurt that I lost my pond but more so hurt at what it symbolized. I spent rest the day filling the hole in the ground he left behind.

In fact, moving on felt like I was filling the holes in my life and in myself he left behind. He was gone, out of my life and took pieces of me that I treasured most, my happiness, my joy, my dreams, confidence, and left empty holes for me to try and fill again. I went to support groups and tried telling my story, but instead I just cried. I tried dating again, but I was just so numb and not opened to anyone "ruining my life again," because that was my mindset. Clearly I couldn't trust myself in picking a good person so I just decided to not even try. Everything I once enjoyed doing became so tarnished by his words, it was hard to find myself enjoying those things either. Even though he was gone, the "damage" had been done and I was lost. At some point I realized that even though he was gone he still had a hold on me.

Here is the honest truth about healing or getting over it. I don't have the answer to that. I know the age old saying of "time will heal all" may have been true. The further removed from the situation I was, the better I felt and although I don't have the answer to how anyone can move on, here are some of the things I had to do. I had to start living life on Mondays and Wednesdays, (he had those days off and I was scared of running into him). I had to go back to training and to doing the things I loved. I hated being single and I had to get back out there, forgive myself for making that horrible choice and have learned to be more careful and take my time. I know there are still things that pop up, some holes I haven't filled all the way. I recently dated a man who asked if I only wear all black. His statement was innocent and inquisitive but my blood boiled and I fired back with, "yes I do and if you have a problem you can leave." So maybe I am still a little sensitive on some matters, but I try and recognize them and I can be open about them or try to not base my reaction on my painful past. There are a lot of important things I learned about relationships that I talk more about in a latter chapter, but I want to share here what helped the most in healing. I didn't want to have negative thoughts towards myself or towards him. In fact, I didn't want to have any negative feelings at all.

As I was moving on I was still scared by what he might try and do to me. I was trying to out-think him so I could try and stay ahead of him. One day I came to the conclusion that I couldn't. I wasn't capable of thinking the way he did. When I realized that I remembered Tiffany's words of "be glad you can't." With those words, my whole attitude changed towards him. I was thankful that I couldn't understand what made someone so hurtful and depraved. Then my heart completely changed to have compassion towards someone who was hurting so much he hurt others. I no longer had negative feelings towards him but I had a heart of compassion towards him. This didn't mean that because I had compassion I would run back to a relationship with him. Having compassion doesn't change how he would treat me, but it did mean I could heal, I could let the negative go and I could replace it with positive energy. Having compassion helped me see that he had to be hurting inside for him to hurt others. He must have felt he had no control in his life in order to try and control me. Instead of judging what he did, I just let myself feel compassion, instead of trying to understand it, I just became thankful I couldn't. When people hurt you it is not a reflection of you but it is the pain they have inside. I have learned that when people lash out at me I meet them with kindness and love and try to help their hurt instead of adding to the pain. I thought learning this was hard, but a true test of having a heart of compassion came a little later in life, and shared a little later in this book.

Learning To Dance
In The Rain

My mom always told me that I can only control myself in this very moment. That was the only thing that I ever had control over in life, myself in that very moment. I may not be able to control what is happening or going on around me but I can control how I react to it or I can control how I feel towards it. I had earlier shared about having a heart of compassion. Learning to have compassion towards a negative person is a way that I have learned to control myself, or control how I view a situation. Sometimes we are in situations we really don't want to be in, but even in that moment we have a choice of how we react to it or feel about it. Even in times of discomfort all we can control is ourselves; we have the choice every single second of every single day to choose how we feel, and to choose our actions. This next story is of a women who felt powerless in her circumstances, but among the storm she learned to dance in the rain.

Ashley Casello

Honestly, I don't even know what happened that night in Vegas. I remember not returning to the hotel room in appropriate amount of time. I remember being accused of flirting with every guy, but you have to believe me, I wasn't. I was helping his inebriated roommate fumble back to the room. I remember him yelling, and I remember him picking her up and throwing her across the room like a rag doll over and over again. I had to do something, I felt so enraged and I just don't know what came over me. I pushed him against the wall and told him, "if you feel like a man hitting girls than hit me!" Next thing I know I am pinned against a chair with his knee in my chest and his hands around my throat. While I was losing oxygen he told me he loved me, he was sorry and he was so messed up in the head. When the police came they kicked him out of the hotel and, against my better judgment, I refused to press charges, after all he loved me and, well, I loved him.

*   *   *   *   *   *   *   *   *   *

Something had never seemed finished in my relationship with the man I thought to be the love of my life. Our relationship had ended, but in my heart it felt we shouldn't have. The first time I met him he worked so hard to pursue me and after he got my attention I fell madly in love for this charming, loving, positive and sociable man. Our relationship was great. We had our ups and downs like every relationship; however, we ended on a bad note. Something in my heart kept telling me to go back, I kept thinking maybe if I tried a little harder, or the timing was better it just might work. I went to his house one night to do his sister's hair, and that night he had me back in his arms. I felt loved again, the way I had felt before, and knew my heart was right about him being the man for me. That moment ended in heartbreak moments later, as I discovered he had a new girlfriend. He told me they weren't going to work out and that he still loved me, his words were sweet but his actions showed otherwise. I watched from a distance as he loved the other woman, and felt like it was pouring salt into an open wound. Those were our favorite restaurants she was enjoying, those were my favorite places he was now sharing with her. Every so often I would hear from him about how horrible the relationship was, how he loved me and wanted out, we would meet only to have him run back to her. The feelings of love became feelings of being used and discarded.

As their relationship began to unravel it was almost as if it was fate. I thought to myself maybe the simple fact was they just weren't meant to be and we were. I thought that when he came to me it was fate bringing us back together for the second chance I had hoped for. Maybe it was love after all and he just needed to fully end it with her to see he loved me. I felt pity for him that he was in such a horrible relationship, with this woman who treated him so badly, and that he was so unhappy. I felt special that he came to me and he would compare me to her and tell me all the ways he felt I was better than her. He told me that he has never loved anyone more than me and that I was the girl for him. I felt flattered, needed and loved. When their relationship finally ended I gladly took my charming man back to give our relationship another go.

I thought that it was going to be the start of my real life fairy tale. We were two lovers separated by circumstances but fate brought us back together. We shared so many fun times and special moments, in a very short time he became by best friend and my confidant. He became my cheerleader and made me believe anything was possible. He had such a positive perspective on life and I just knew he was the guy I needed in my life. He made me feel so beautiful and worthy, things that I hadn't felt in such a long time. I had given up all hope that there were any good guys left and he restored my faith in men, and love and then we went to Vegas...

Honesty, I don't know what happened that night. I remember bits and pieces but ask for a time line or a story, all I can say was it was unbelievable. To the point I didn't want to believe it happened. After I gave him the keys to my car he continued to message me through the night, coming up with every excuse possible for his behavior and begged me to forgive him. The next day I hung out at the pool and waited for him to finish work so we could take the long drive back. That was the longest most awkward four hours of my life. No one said a single word to each other and you could cut the tension in the car with a knife. When I got home I didn't speak a word of it to anyone. Maybe because I was in such disbelief that it had happened, maybe I was embarrassed. I know I didn't tell my parents out of fear of what they would do or the sadness that their baby had been hurt, maybe it was to protect him, or maybe it was just to protect me from how others would react. It ate at me for weeks and I finally told my boss, who of course, told me I needed to leave him. She asked if this was the first time it had happened and informed me that things normally don't get better and usually get worse. Her words gave me the courage, so I blocked all forms of communication with him and moved on with my life, never to look back. If only that last part were true.

Three months of peace, and time spent with my family, then one night at 3:00 A.M. a knock at my door woke me up. Standing at the door in tears and with a sad story, was the ghost who loved me with his hands around my throat. As he stood at the door in the cold, I heard the story of how he had changed and how sorry he was. He promised everything under the sun, that he would love me right, the way I should be loved. Also, nothing like what had happen in Vegas would ever happen again. Being the sucker I was for our true love conquers all story, and because he loved me, I gave him a second (third) chance. I was so glad I did. Mr. Wonderful was back in my life. He treated me so well, he was once again the prince of a man I initially thought him to be. He was on such good behavior, I was convinced the incident in Vegas was just a bad moment in time, a random drunken act of jealousy, a mistake, a moment of weakness. Everyone has them, we are human. We all make mistakes. So I felt I did the right thing by forgiving him and taking him back.

Roses on our monthly anniversaries, special nights out, coming out to flowers he left on my car while I was at work, little love notes hidden all over my room for me to find, I felt like the luckiest girl alive. After the Vegas incident he had to win the approval of my family, who were my everything. He did whatever he had to do to get them to like him again. Like when he knew I was with them he would text me with things that would make me smile. He advised me that the best way to convince people that I was happy was the always show them I was happy when I left his house. He and I worked hard to get them to accept our relationship and to accept him back into their lives. Although they never truly accepted him and fell for his game, they pretended to, to make me happy. It seemed the second he got their approval, the man in the Vegas hotel room showed up again. He knew I wouldn't be able to tell my parents or family that Dr. Jekyll had turned back into Mr. Hyde, because I just spent months trying to convince them he had changed. I would have been a liar, and I had to save face and keep whatever little dignity I had left. Instead of letting them see his true colors, I covered for him. I put on a fake smile, spoke only of the good times (like he told me to do) and would only cry alone. It was like I was living a double life.

When he and I were good, we were really good. It was fun and simply the best time and feeling in the world. But when it was bad, it was really bad. He was a jealous person and I would find myself changing things about myself to hopefully not "set him off." He hated some of my clothes, so to keep the peace I would make sure I wore only the clothes he approved of. I wasn't even suppose to wear a bikini at the beach because he said I was asking for guys to look at me. If I wasn't off work at the exact time I was supposed to be (and my job required me to stay late at times), he would accuse me of cheating or talking to someone else. If I ran errands after work, it would be a fight about why it took me so long to get home, so I made sure, immediately after work, to go straight home. I longed for those good times and felt if I would just watch what I did, mind how I acted or refrained from anything I thought he wouldn't approve of, maybe there would be peace that night and maybe it would be a good night. Those nights that were good made my heart so happy, but I learned after a while, that no matter what I did or how I acted, those good nights became fewer and farther between.

I couldn't seem to do anything right, I couldn't pick the right clothes, I didn't have the right answers, everything seemed to always be my fault, everything was a fight and every night seemed to be a fight about something new. I slowly started becoming withdrawn from everything and everyone who I loved and who loved me, trying to hide the pain and the confusion in my eyes. I began avoiding my closest friends not only because I didn't want to tell them the truth about my relationship and because I was embarrassed and ashamed but I also couldn't believe I was allowing this in my life. My happy bubbly existence was starting to fizzle.

If it was so bad, why didn't I just leave, you ask? I tried, all the time! When I would walk away he would come running back as the nice, sweet loveable guy who I truly loved. He would bring me flowers and tell me how much he loved me and I would just melt and fall for it. Every time I tried to leave he would say, "we are better than this". He always knew *exactly* what to say to get me back in his arms. When all else failed, he would tell me he was going to kill himself, or some other dramatic form of pity and I just couldn't have that on my hands so I would take him back. It was a game, a vicious cycle that I could not stop playing. I kept picking up the same deck of cards, shuffling them and hoped to find the king. Also, I was hopeful that one day I would wake up and miraculously he would be that nice, lovable, sweet sociable guy I fell in love with. The longer I stayed away from family and friends the further down the rabbit hole I went. With no one to confide in, he convinced me that the fighting and the chaos was normal in relationships and that I was lucky to be with him.

Since I had withdrawn from the world, I spent a lot of time on the internet and I came across an article written by the woman he was with before me. I was looking on her Facebook page to see if he had been talking to her again or to see if she had posted anything about him. Since he had cheated on her with me, a part of me knew that he might cheat on me. I saw a link to an article titled, "Out of the Darkness." With that title, I just *had* to read it and had to see if it was about him. All I knew about this woman was, according to him, she was crazy, treated him poorly, and left him on the side of the road after he had been beaten up one night. She was also clearly not over him as she had spray painted her name on the wall of his house, mailed him a love quote from Grays Anatomy and had taped their pictures to the door at his work. I couldn't imagine what she could have possibly written about him. I began to read the article and quickly got a different impression of her. She was over him, very much so, and as I read more I began to see her story in my life. She had mentioned that he began to tear down the essence of who she was and as I reflected on that, I barely recognized the women who I had become. The article made me see that I wasn't alone. Someone else has stood in my shoes, someone else knew exactly how I was feeling, and although I didn't know her I felt connected to her. It also really opened my eyes to what was going on in my relationship; this type of behavior wasn't normal or acceptable. I was being abused and treated wrongly. I showed him the article and like everything else, he manipulated me into thinking it was the proof that she wasn't over him. He claimed that she made these lies up because she was bitter that HE left HER. I somewhat believed his manipulation but her words were always in the back of my head and it seemed that my eyes had been opened a little to his games. I saw his actions and heard her words. When he would yell at me I would say to myself "this is what she meant by being torn down, this is what she meant by everything she loved being stripped away." It was happening to me before my very eyes but yet I still loved him and hoped for that miracle morning.

A miracle morning did happen one day, but in the form of a new life growing inside me. I found out I was pregnant! I had always wanted to be a mom, it was a dream come true and I hoped that this little miracle would be the reason I would also get my miracle with him. Maybe for her he would miraculously change and put Mr. Hyde away for good. It seemed though, once I found out I was pregnant he thought he had a hold on me and that I would never leave. What I could never imagine as getting worse was like a bad dream turning into a nightmare. I thought things were bad, but I found out there was room for things to get worse as he repeatedly struck me in the head with his fist. He had put his hands on me in the past, but now it wasn't only my safety at risk, I had a new life growing in me that I also had to protect. I went to the police and he was arrested. The police gave me a restraining order so he could never contact me again. I was relieved that I was going to have a safe and calm pregnancy and I wasn't going to subject my child to that type of life style. Still trapped in this game, I still worried at the thought of him sitting in jail or getting beat up but I made up my mind and I was going to raise this baby all on my own. Shortly after, I was feeling alone and missing him, after all he was the father of this child I was carrying. Maybe she would be the miracle that could change him. Maybe she would be the reason he changed. I know I thought it before but before he couldn't see her or hold her. One night late in my room, against his restraining order, I received a message from him, the charming sweet man, the Dr. Jekyll, the man I loved. He convinced me to meet him and to let him talk to me in person. I wanted the fairy tale family and the happy ending so, with hope in my heart, I went to meet him to see what he had to say. Of course, you can guess, with my history with him, his words sounded so sweet, like honey on my lips, or maybe it was his kiss that was sweet but either way I fell for his venomous words. We gave it another chance.

The day of my delivery came and went. My beautiful happy baby was finally here. She brought so much joy to my life and at first glance I felt what true love felt like. Like every mother says their baby is perfect, but looking at mine I knew that statement was true. He also looked at her with love and I felt that I was right. She would be the miracle that changed him. I was so happy to be a first time mom, and that the love of my life stepped up to the plate and became the guy I just knew he could be.

Like everything else and every single time in our relationship the prince charming was only there for a few weeks or so. Soon after we took the baby home he had little to no interest in being in her life. He would get frustrated when she cried and handed her back to me. He had more important things to do such as riding and even signed up for four weekend races which meant his days off were spent riding his bike, rather than see her. In the first month I was already begging him to come spend time with her. If you followed his social media pages you would have thought otherwise. He would show up long enough to take pictures with her, post about how much he loved her, play the father of the year roll just enough for everyone to see, then left to go about his day. It was frustrating and although I wanted him in my life out of fear of being lonely, I came to realize it was even lonelier being with him. I was stuck now. He was the father of my child and I had to try and make it work for her sake.

We would go to doctors appointments together, here and there. He would take us to dinner to "get me out of the house", but only on such an occasion he had nothing better to do; he would take me out long enough to get his "happy family" picture, but it was back to his old antics of yelling and screaming at me. I remember my poor baby getting a diaper rash and having to hear how I was the worse mother on the planet for not taking care of her the way he thought I should. Do I need to mention that he had only changed maybe two or three diapers since she had been born? Not only that, but I was doing everything I could to take care of my baby and I was a darn good mother. I know that now, but in the moment, I let his words get to me. One day, in the middle of us arguing, he grabbed the baby and looked into her face and told her how much he hated me. He looked at my baby and with a sweet voice he told her, "Mommy is a (insert a very vulgar word that starts with a C has a U and ends with NT), is coo coo and needs medication." I had had enough! Some may say I lost my mind, others think I acted as anyone else would act in that situation. I got up and went to get my baby to leave. He stood up and was holding her yelling at me that I wasn't going to take the baby. My poor little girl started screaming and crying with all the yelling. She was scared and so was I. With him holding my screaming child, calling me names and threatening to never give the baby back, I reacted as I feel anyone would have. I called my dad to come help me get the baby and to help me leave his house. He had no regard for the child he was holding; it was just another part of his twisted game of manipulation, abuse and control. And that, my friends, was the straw that broke the camel's back.

For real this time, there was no going back! He wasn't going to change, this was the life that she and I were going to live for the rest of our lives and I couldn't take another minute of it. I had been through hell with this guy and I wasn't going to let her experience a single second more of it. My precious eight week old baby didn't need to hear that type of language or hear someone talk to her mother that way. I may have not been strong enough to leave him in the past but I had a much more important reason to leave now and that was my daughter.

I sat in my room and cried with sickness. *How did it get so bad? How was I so stupid to keep going back and to allow this in my life. This wasn't who I was.* I was once a strong confident woman, who had been broken down to a scared and timid woman who lacked any sort of self worth. I sat there and didn't know a single person I could talk to. I had lied to everyone about how wonderful my relationship was and I had pretty much pulled away from all my friends and family. I didn't know who I could talk to and felt no one would understand how I felt, *where would I go? Who could I talk to?* Then I remembered there was one person who knew exactly how I felt. His ex. I was feeling remorse for being that girl, for believing his lies and felt an overwhelming urge to reach out to her, hoping maybe she could help me. The story of what happened when I reached out comes in the next chapter but this story isn't over.

Even though I was out of the relationship, the mental and emotional abuse continued because he now had rights to continue to talk to me and visitations with my daughter, which negated the restraining order we had previously established. I was continuously agitated, endless questions swirling around in my mind: *How can I heal from abuse if I'm continually experiencing it? How does any loving mother just hand a helpless child over to a person who is so dark and ugly? How do I escape the madness when the madness is surrounding me? How do I escape the toxicity when I am unwillingly exposed to it?* As the visitations started, his games became even more depraved because they involved my baby girl. One day I tried to reschedule his visitation because she was too sick. He waited until 9:00 p.m. to have the cops make me wake my sick baby for a two hour visit with him. My only guess is he did this to show me he still had control. He saw her for 20 minutes and gave her back saying it was too late for her to be out. After consulting my legal resources I now understand a police officer wouldn't give false information or call a single mother and threaten to take her child away under this circumstance, like the supposed police officer did that night.

After a visit one night, he advised me she had a scratch on her foot (possibly caused from her nails), and "don't worry, I took a picture of it ". My first thought went down the dark alley of how he had something on me, and subsequently he's going to try and take the baby away. Very quickly I took control of my thoughts and realized that during his visits with her, he looked for things against me and all he could find was the tiniest scratch. Instead of him cutting her nails to prevent future scratches he just took a picture. If a scratch here and a scratch there is all he has on me, I am doing a darn good job! *Lord knows there is plenty more where that came from!*

Handing my precious baby over to him for a few hours a week made me sick. For a brief moment, I even considered enduring the darkness by staying in a relationship with this person just so I could have an illusion of control and maybe even being able to better protect my daughter. I quickly came to my senses, realizing that staying with him would mean that my life would be unbearable and that my ability to keep her safe around him would actually be lessened. In the grand scheme of things, a few long hours per week is better than 168 hours per week.

I became consumed with trying to stay one step ahead of him. I felt like I needed to out-think him by trying to predict his next act of malice. I tried to anticipate what he would say or what he would do. I laid in bed at night paralyzed in fear at the thought that he could convince the world that he was really Dr. Jeckyl and that I was the bad person. When we had to correspond, I would try to anticipate how he would use my reply against me, if I didn't reply I had to think of how he would use my non responsiveness against me. I was trapped in fear and anxiety of his next move. The fear I experienced was not for me but for my child. Being a mother, all you want is the best for your child, and you want to protect her and keep her safe. I felt powerless, controlled by him, and still very much trapped. As I continued to try and out-think him, or try and stay one step ahead of him, I learned that there was no out-thinking someone as dark as he. Trying to think like him appeared to be a logical strategy but in reality I needed to put aside all logic to think in his world of manipulation and depravity. I could never play the sick and twisted game on his level and when I realized that, I decided I didn't want to.

His insanity became my insanity until I made the choice to return to rational/healthy thinking. Not letting him affect me anymore was an easy decision to make. Putting that into practice is easier said than done, but I needed to start somewhere. Nothing was going to change with him, so the change had to begin with me. The definition of insanity is doing the same thing over and over expecting a different result, so I had to get off the merry go round and leave the insanity to him. The first step for me was realizing that I had to stop reacting to him. I had to stop letting him get to me. At first I thought, "at least he doesn't know I am reacting so he doesn't think he won." The game had to stop being about him and had to start being about my health, my peace and my sanity. He didn't know he was getting the reaction out of me but I was still reacting. I had to learn to sincerely not react.

When you start to take control of your own thoughts and your reactions, you begin to take control of your life. Learning not to react isn't an overnight, one decision kind of fix. It is a constant choice. The biggest change came when I stopped thinking about him and redirected my focus to myself and my daughter. I started to regain my confidence. I am a good mother and any educated healthy person would see that. While his actions, at times, affect me, they have nothing to do with me.

It's taken me a while to get to this realization and honestly, I know I have a long road ahead for healing and finding the confidence I used to have. As soon as I made the initial choice to not let him affect me, the best strategy was learning to control myself. I can't control anyone else. I might influence someone, but I can only control me. AND I can only control myself in the "now". Getting lost in what he might or could do robbed me of the "now" of my life. I also realize that my life is more than the white noise that he causes in my head. It's an exhausting process, but I love myself more and more every day, especially when I see the way my daughter looks at me. She needs me. She adores me. Despite what I believed of myself before she came along, I have so much to offer her. I know healing me is what my daughter needs most. I am a woman, mother and a role model to my daughter. Understanding my value as a woman and demonstrating healthy behaviors provides her the best opportunity for a mutually beneficial loving adult relationship.

I will no longer wake up each morning and wonder what kind of storm it will be. I could anticipate a hail storm, but that day comets would fall from the sky. Some days I was ready for a hurricane and it was bright and sunny. I realized that because I was always looking for the storms, I wasn't enjoying the sunshine. I will no longer allow my mind to be consumed by him or the darkness associated by him. Trying to think like him very well could have landed me in an insane asylum. By trying to out-think insanity, my mind was no better than his and he still had the control. I had to find a way to dance in the rain, a way to break free and reclaim both myself and the positive light in my life. Every time I looked at my smiling sweet baby girl, my world was sunny and my heart was happy. I had to learn to stay in those happy moments and not let the thoughts of him creep in and have any piece of my joy. My baby girl is growing so fast and I don't want to waste a minute of her precious childhood in worry and fear! I had to accept that he is going to continue to do manipulative things (to me, to my daughter and the world around him). He is going to lie, manipulate, cheat, and do unhealthy things, and no matter how much I worry or plan, it isn't going to change. I had to get out of the way and allow God to be God. I know the saying, "you can only control yourself in this moment." All I can do is control myself and only in this moment. I had to take the control back. Did I want him to control my thoughts or did I want to be free? The choice is mine and I choose freedom.

Walk Each Other Home

I mentioned earlier in this book that my greatest opportunity to show compassion would come later. This was a chance to put into practice what I had learned and ironically from the same situation. Although we have already talked about not judging people and meeting them on an emotional level, there is something else I would like you to get from the story I am about to share. I would like to share what happens when we use our experiences and help others. In life, we go through some seasons of stormy weather, difficult times and hard lessons learned. Sometimes we go through those hard lessons and wish we had someone to help us through. Hopefully when you have weathered the storm you have learned valuable lessons. You may have learned a lesson of how not to get into a particular storm, lessons of how to dance in the storm, or lessons on how to rebuild after it. These lessons are valuable and the impact you can have on someone's life by sharing these lessons can be monumental. You can help prevent pain, help ease sorrow, give hope, give a hug of understanding. You can be the person that you might have wished you had to help you. It is my belief that when we go through a storm, it is for us to grow, but I also believe we are on this planet to help each other along the way as well.

If you haven't already realized, Ashley was the other women in my story and I am the "crazy ex" in her story. She mentioned in her story she was sitting in her room one night, alone, desperate and scared with no one to turn to. She remembered my article and that I had gone through the same things so she decided to reach out to me. We pick up this story with her making the decision to reach out to me, told from both our perspectives.

Jeneae Noonan

Ashley Casello

Ashley:

I was feeling remorse for being "that girl", for believing his lies and felt an overwhelming feeling to reach out to her, hoping she'd forgive me, even hoping maybe, she could help me. I sat alone in my room one night while my sweet baby was sleeping and began pouring my heart out to this complete stranger. We may have known of each other but never knew each other and being that I was the other women in their relationship, I could only imagine how she felt about me. *What if she is as crazy as he made her to be? What if I send this letter and she tells me I deserve to be where I am at? What if she confirms my worry that this is just karma biting me in the butt? What if reaching out to her just makes me feel guiltier, but could I really feel any worse?* With these questions racing through my mind I continued to pour my heart out to her. A part of me saw a different woman from what I had come to believe about her in her article. She didn't write the article to hurt him, but to help others, she clearly knew exactly where I was at and maybe, just maybe she could have compassion for the situation. I read the letter a few times over, crossed my fingers, hoping I was right about her and he was wrong, took a deep breath and sent the letter.

*   *   *   *   *   *   *   *   *   *

Jenae:

I remember sitting on the couch on a Friday night watching Ancient Aliens, my typical Friday night treat, when my messenger went off. I remember thinking who would message me at 11:30, at night, on a Friday. I looked down and saw a familiar face of someone, not a friend but of someone who, I hate to admit, I had only been Facebook stalking for a good year or so. My heart pounding through my chest, my mouth got dry and I got sick to my stomach. *What possibly could the woman who was with my ex possible want from me? Was this part of a sick game that he was continuing to play?* My roommate grabbed my phone. With the look on my face and how I was reacting he could only assume it was a message from the ex himself. It took a second to calm myself down and although my roommate tried to have me not read the message, curiosity won me over and I read the message. After picking my jaw up from the floor it was not the message I was expecting at all.

At first I wanted to tell her "you made this bed you lay in it," but it's a good thing I have a sensor and patiently thought out my reply. As I read the letter the third and fourth time, my heart began to feel a familiar brokenness. I saw a broken person, reaching out to someone, who she only knew was crazy, for forgiveness. Furthermore, I saw a woman so broken that she felt this was her punishment or, as she had called it, Karma. I saw a woman so beaten and broken down that she reached out to someone who could very well have hated her, hoping I didn't, hoping for forgiveness, and knowing I might be the only one who could relate to where she was and how she was feeling. I saw me, two years ago. Or to be honest I wasn't sure if she had known why she wrote to me but I saw a woman in pain and I knew, first hand, exactly how she felt, standing in those same shoes just a few months back. In my most honest fashion, I told her I didn't hate her and that I was glad for her because she took this monster out of my life. I told her that no one deserves to go through what she is going through and because I knew firsthand the terror, the sickness, the sadness and the madness, that I would be there for her. I assured her that she was not alone and that I can give her support. At first I was scared, me myself still trapped by this guy's control two years later. *What if he found out I was talking to her? Would he try and come after me? Would I hear from him?* I was scared of what he might do and in a moment of bravery I thought to myself "no I will no longer allow him to control me, I will be there for her and if I hear from him I will remind him he has no business talking to me." I had written that article to be of help to anyone who might need it and had helped a few other women that had reached out to me, why should she be any different, just because I had a past with the abuser? I sent the letter and waited to hear back.

*   *   *   *   *   *   *   *   *   *

Ashley:

When I saw her reply I had to take a minute before I even opened it. *Did I want to know what she had to say? Was I really ready to be told off? This was my Karma I had to face the bullet.* I began to read the letter. The first sentence said, "I don't hate you I was thankful for you," was that a jab? Was she saying I deserved this? I was right, this was what I deserved, but then I continued reading. She didn't hated me and she expressed she understood and she was willing to be there for me. I felt a sense of relief; here was someone who knew what I was going through and was willing to help me. I wasn't alone after all and she was someone I could be honest about the relationship with, because she had been there too. I poured my heart out a little more to her and actually got a few laughs in that night. We compared stories, most of which were the exact same. We made jokes about spray paint and love notes. Most importantly, that night I gained a comrade, a friend, and a confidant.

*   *   *   *   *   *   *   *   *   *

Jenae:

I believe that night Ashley and I spoke till about 3 am. Mostly I listened; I assured her she wasn't alone in the way she was feeling or alone in the situation. That was the first time where my terrifying circumstance finally had meaning. As much as I was there for Ashley, she was there for me. There were things in me that began to heal that night. It had come full circle. Every fear, every sick feeling, every painful moment now helped me understand her need and I was able help her. As much credit as she gives me for being there for her, she helped me heal as well. Together we grew, together we got through this.

The most powerful moment for me was the day of her restraining order case. I had told her in the beginning I would be there for her and that meant that day as well. I knew I would see him, or better yet he would see me. I really had to look deep inside myself and check my motives. I wanted to be there for her and that was a pure enough motive for me. I had some fears the night before, but knew that that moment would be a powerful statement. I went to court with her and made the statement that together we are strong and together we are standing up to you.

Like I said earlier, we all have our trials and can use them in a positive way. We can guide others, we can hold someone's hand, we can even just lend a supportive ear. We can give someone hope in a moment we might have felt hopeless ourselves. One of my favorite saying is "we are all just walking each other home" by Ram Dass. Wouldn't it be better to hold someone's hand in the process?

Lessons We Came Away With

Ashley and I wrote from a heart of wanting to help anyone who might find themselves in a similar situation. We thought it would be even more helpful to point out a few things to watch out for. So, here are a few things we have learned. Note: because we are ladies who have experienced this with a man we are going to refer to the abusive individual as "he"; however, ladies are just as capable of this behavior too so it can go either way.

Set good boundaries, and stick to them. I know when I first met the guy, I allowed my boundaries to be tested and pushed around. If you know what you will and won't stand for in a relationship keep those boundaries tight. The first time a boundary is pushed, the next becomes easier to be pushed. If a person isn't willing to respect your boundaries, you do not need them in your life.

Be Honest with yourself. If you feel that you have to lie about your relationship, or you have to keep your relationship a secret, it is most likely not a healthy relationship. Ashley felt the need to make the relationship look good and lied about how bad things really were. When she needed help, she felt alone because at that point she felt everyone she knew had a different picture about the relationship. She made it seem perfect, who would believe otherwise? It is important to be honest with yourself and others. If you feel you can't tell people what is really going on, it might be time to get out.

Everyone is Crazy. I laugh at this one, but it's true. If, from your significant others perspective, all his ex's are crazy, there might be something wrong with him and you will be the next "crazy one." If the new person has stories of all the wrong their ex did to them, or how bad their ex was, listen to see if they are playing the victim. At least when I talk about this certain ex, I can mention things I did wrong and he is the only ex I refer to as crazy. If all the ex's are crazy from his stand point, that is a very good clue that you are dealing with a narcissist.

He doesn't really like you. Looking back I can laugh at this one too. I dated a guy who didn't like a single thing about me. He hated my job, the way I dressed, the things I loved and wanted to mold me to what he liked. Why be with someone who doesn't actually like who you are? If you find yourself changing things so this person will like you and treat you better, the relationship isn't healthy. There is someone out there who will love you for who you are right now, and you don't need to change a thing to make anyone happy or to make someone like you.

Negative communication. I have a bible verse from Corinthians on my ribs that includes, "love is kind." If the person who is supposed to love you isn't kind, especially with his words, then it isn't love. No one on this planet should use their words to degrade you, humiliate you, insult you or hurt you in any way. Emotional and verbal abuse leaves deeper scars than some physical abuse. When you leave an abusive relationship, the hitting stops but the damage the words do, takes a very long time to heal. People can get angry and say things they don't mean on occasion, but if this is a pattern or a daily form of communication, this person doesn't love you the way they say they do and there is someone else out there who can truly love you. It is a hurt and unhealthy person who hurt others, "hurt people hurt people," and the words this person uses are a mere reflection of the lack of love they have for themselves. Often times they take it out on anyone else but themselves.

For the friends and family. Some signs that a loved one is being abused are they might withdraw from people and things they love. In an abusive relationship, the abuser will vocally disapprove of things your loved one likes and to save from the argument they may stop doing that activity all together. Also, as hard as it may be, if you observe them in an abusive relationship, pressuring them to leave won't help the cause. When they have had enough, they will leave. What helps though, is being an ear they can talk to. Let them know they are being hurt, let them know they are being treated wrongly. Most importantly, listen. Be a safe place they can go. Love is blind in some cases and in Ashley's and my case we were definitely blinded by love. I was thankful to have open communication with my parents. Seeing their baby hurting, hurt them, but my mom thought if she put too much pressure on me to leave him, I might choose him over her (until we are ready to leave, we tend to defend the abuser). When speaking with her, she would say things like, "things will only get worse. I am sorry he treats you so bad. How will this change?" She asked me one day, if I would bring a child into a relationship like that and if my answer was no, "why would I waste more time with him?" What helped me see I needed out was her actually making me see it for myself. Her asking the questions that would get me thinking. She never shamed me or made he feel embarrassed. There was enough of that going on already. She just made it very clear she wanted better for my life and helped me see with my own eyes, the true colors of the relationship.

"Let Go and Let God"

Have you ever had a dream that you wouldn't let anyone get in the way of? Earlier in this book we talked about never letting anyone get in your way and to push for your dreams as much as you can. Ironically though, sometimes the person standing in your way is you. It could be your doubting thoughts, your concrete plans, your stubborn ways, or all of the above. You know you want the gift behind door number one that you bang your head against it hoping it will open not realizing door two also leads there. Sometimes when you have beaten all options down (it's the fighter in me) it might be best to let go and let God. I am sure you have heard that one before, but it is true. Sometimes the obstacle getting in the way of achieving our goals is ourselves. We have a dream we want to achieve, but we are so stuck in our own planning that we either don't see an easier way or we keep knocking on the same door waiting for it to open. I am a firm believer in having a dream and working towards it and doing whatever it takes but am also open to seeing other ways of achieving it. Having a plan is good, but being flexible is going to save you a lot of heartache.

I know personally when I have a dream and it isn't working out the way I have planned, I feel that it never will work out and I feel that this moment is the way things will be forever. Usually in those moments of panic or those moments of disappointment, I go into over drive with my panicking and scheming. I would beat down the doors because they weren't opening fast enough or I thought the only way to get the door to open was to beat it down. Funny thing happens when you take a step back and see the sign next to the door that says "turn the handle counter clockwise." In those moments you have to get out of your own way and let God take the wheel. He knows your plan. He knows your heart. He will get you there. It might not be in *your* time line but as Amy P showed us earlier is there is no better timing than God's.

I have known this next author my whole life and some of the facts in this upcoming story were even shocking to me. She had big plans in her life and marriage and they were not going her way. When she hits the road block, she looks to everyone else for help to move it, only to discover that she, herself, is the roadblock.

Tiffany Avans

Growing up in a broken home and seeing the world around me, I imagined that marriage would be challenging. It took less than two years for the struggle I had anticipated, to become my reality. My husband had failed to meet my expectations on multiple levels and my marriage of two long years was riddled with addictions, disappointment, chaos, infidelity and we were hanging by a thread. I thought being married would mean that I would never have to be alone and here I was married and had never felt more alone in my life.

With our inability to agree on finances and many other important decisions grownups have to make, my dreams of being happily married, owning a home and becoming a mother were seemingly impossible. Clearly I had made a mistake and it was not going to work out between us. I was still young and it wasn't too late for me to start over and find real happiness that I deserved, with someone who would treat me right, make good choices and meet my expectations. Parting ways and cutting our losses was the only option.

Everything seemed to be going perfectly for everyone around me with beautiful weddings, happy marriages, babies on the way, home ownership and a real "happily ever after". I was blessed to celebrate their happiness and joy, but couldn't help but feel the pain, heartache, embarrassment, sadness and shame that come with the monstrous marital challenges I was facing.

<u>ONCE UPON A TIME</u>

It was a crisp January afternoon. I had just finished finals for the first semester of my senior year. I was meeting a friend at a house when in walked this extremely striking boy with dark hair, the most piercing blue eyes I had ever seen, fair skin, walked with noticeable confidence and all I could think was, "WOW!" The second I laid eyes on him it was immediate fireworks and there was no denying the physical attraction we had for each other. In my seventeen year old mind he was "so cute" and I needed to know anything and everything I could about this boy! After spending a full day with Ryan, I went home and gushed in my journal about how gorgeous he was and how he made me laugh. We were fast friends and it didn't take long before I felt the love and affection I craved from him. For the first time in a long time I felt wanted and appreciated. I was smitten!

The last months of my senior year were spent looking forward to a future with him but we didn't know the first thing about being grownups yet, which made our young love very complicated. We went to my Sadie Hawkins and Senior Prom together; it was always the best time when I was with him. But that ended abruptly when he broke up with me the day after my 18th birthday. I was devastated and confused as I didn't want to be alone and I truly felt that we were supposed to be together. I quickly pulled it together knowing that I was young, starting college and had a lot to learn about myself, life, love, and responsibility.

I didn't see or hear from him after our breakup. I spent my time going to class, working hard, playing hard and dating here and there. All the while, it felt like God was pointing His fingers for Ryan and I to at least know each other. Every so often I would bump into his mom at the mall or a restaurant. She made sure to mention that he hadn't dated anyone since me and that "he still cares for you". She told Ryan about her encounters with me and told him "she still cares about you" (thanks for being a matchmaker mom!) I saw him at a pool hall one time and despite the fact that I was in a relationship at that point, it was really exciting to see him. I felt the same butterflies I did when I was 17 years old. Every so often we would connect via instant messenger and when I saw his name, it made my heart race. Our time together was unforgettable and I very much longed for that with him again.

REKINDLE

Almost six years after our break up, we scheduled a coffee date. The days leading up to that, we decided to do dinner instead. That dinner turned into him picking me up. I changed my outfit about five times before I realized how excited I really was. That night after dinner, we reaffirmed our affections for one another and decided to rekindle the flame that was once before. We immediately discussed marriage. We told our family and friends we were getting married. I remember my mom asking me, "why do you want to marry Ryan?"

I think I said something like "he makes me laugh, I love him, he loves me and he will make beautiful babies!"

She asked, "will he be a good father?" I hadn't thought that far ahead but I knew our babies would be gorgeous if they looked anything like him.

Our physical and emotional connection was undeniable, but a lot can change in 6 years. One of our challenges was that we were still in love with the idea of being in love with the people we used to be. Now we were both a little different. I liked to get out and socialize but he was more of a homebody. The first few months we spent a lot of time doing what I wanted and Ryan quickly discovered that I have no "off switch". He put his foot down and started telling me "no". I thought couples were supposed to do things together and I took it personal when he would "blow me off". It was disappointing when social engagements would come up and I had to attend alone. Often times I was too embarrassed and would just not go so I didn't have to explain why I was there alone. When I did go and questions were asked, I felt embarrassed because there was no good excuse and I am not a good liar. I tried to put on a good show. I wanted everything to look good from the outside.

Those first few months we drank a lot together. When he was drunk, his behavior and language were hurtful and he betrayed my trust. I never before thought I would put up with that kind of treatment but I loved him so much. I didn't want to be alone, I felt like we were supposed to be together and that we could nip this thing in the bud and so I stayed. Like a sweet and loving girlfriend, when he did something wrong I would keep it in my back pocket and use it as ammo when it was convenient for me. I would hope that he felt so much remorse that he would want to be a better and different man after that.

Our first New Year's Eve, he was hell bent on spending it the same way he and the boys always spent New Year's Eve, at the pool hall. I didn't want to go, but there was no negotiating; his mind had been made up, plans were in motion and I wasn't going to miss our first new year's eve (even if I wasn't invited). We all drank too much and I didn't fancy his behavior. He wasn't paying enough attention to me. After the countdown, on our way to the car he had a friend on each side helping him to stay vertical. Feeling justified in my anger and disappointments of the night (and with clouded judgment myself) I kicked him from behind. I thought he was so drunk he wouldn't remember anything, so I slapped him across the face to make him feel my pain. Still hanging on his friends, he kicked me in the stomach. Conveniently taking advantage of the fact that he wouldn't remember he was provoked I let the story unfold as such... He woke up on New Year's Day wondering what happened. His friend told him that he had kicked me in the stomach. He blew up my phone with dozens of sobbing messages apologizing profusely. I let him feel sorry, ashamed, devastated at the thought of losing me. I let it drag on for several days. Thanks to my distortion of the truth, he decided to stay "dry" after that incident realizing that alcohol was not a good idea. Because he seemed sincerely remorseful and swore to change his ways, I took him back.

Since I was willing to stay with him, I expected him to become a "better man" and do everything in his power to make it up to me. I wanted more than anything to get married, start a family and to secure my future of never being alone. I was less than subtle about wanting to be married. We had talked about marriage and we told our families we were going to get married but after a year of talking about it, being together, and "putting up with all the crap", we were now living together, there was no ring on my finger, no wedding to plan and I was getting restless.

ENGAGED

We had been dating for about 16 months when Ryan took me hot air ballooning for my 25th birthday. That morning, standing in the basket of a hot air balloon floating in the sky, I found a sign down below that said "TIFFANY WILL YOU MARRY ME?" I looked over at him to see a princess cut diamond ring and a smile on his face. Of course I said "Yes!" Now that I had a ring on my finger I could plan a wedding, we could start our marriage and my dreams of being a wife, mother and homeowner were well on their way.

One cold hard fact we faced in our new engagement was that Ryan's mom was very sick. She had been battling lung cancer for over a year and it had grown in her body. We had to decide between a long engagement or quick one so mom could be present for the wedding. Financially, we were ill prepared to be married and independent but we decided to marry right away.

After a week of being engaged, we set the date. My mom took me dress shopping. I will never forget my sister-in-law wheeling my mother-in-law and her one year old daughter into the bridal store so we could pick out the dress. I tried on several dresses but the second I put on the big poufy princess dress, my mother-in-law choked up and we all had a moment, you know the one where you need to pass around the Kleenex. That was the one. I called my dad and said, "Dad, what are you doing in two weeks? Can you get a tux and walk me down the aisle?" I called my best friend the Tuesday before the wedding and said "what are you doing on Sunday? Can you pick up a dress and be in our wedding?"

THE WEDDING

On August 26th, 2007, after our three week engagement our wedding day arrived. We originally planned on getting married in the same church Ryan's parents were married in but my mother-in-law's health declined quickly and she was on hospice at home just four days before the wedding. We moved the location to the backyard of the home where Ryan grew up (and also the home where we met). They rolled my mother-in-law out in her hospital bed and she had the best seat in the house. As I walked down the aisle I remember my feelings of hope and excitement sitting in the shadow of fear and uncertainty. *What if he starts drinking again? What if this is a mistake?* In the back of my mind divorce was an option. Part of me hoped that despite the truth that marriage does not change personalities and priorities that this would somehow be a new beginning for us and that we could conquer some of the "big deals" we had been sweeping under the rug. We exchanged traditional vows in a very intimate ceremony before God, close family and friends. With tremendous help from my mom, my sister-in-law and several friends, it was the perfect day. Sadly, my sweet mother-in-law passed away just three days after the wedding. It has always made our anniversary bittersweet.

HONEYMOON - TROUBLE IN PARADISE

Just one week after we were married I was laid off. After a couple months of job searching, I found a new job. Before we had celebrated six months of marriage, we had both been laid off (me for a second time). It was not looking good for us. We were living with his dad, both unemployed and we had a lot of debt. We had intended to "save money" and get out of debt; however, it didn't take a rocket scientist to see the financial decisions we were making to contradict that intention. Our first year of marriage, after we had both been laid off and were living off of unemployment checks, we took a honeymoon to Kauai and spent our one year anniversary in Costa Rica. They were both great trips and as irresponsible as it was I am glad we went... But still...

We experienced a tough combination of outside circumstances and poor decisions on our part. My personal insecurities quickly surfaced. I dreaded the question "how is married life!?" Friends and family inquired with high hopes for us. I would smile and try to be as general as possible as I didn't want to sabotage my image and any little dignity we had left. In my mind he was doing everything wrong. I lacked patience and faith and our circumstance already felt hopeless. *This marriage is terrible and is going to be like this forever!* He was spending too much money on things that didn't matter. He was spending too much time on his computer (and obviously not enough with me). He was starting to experiment with mind altering substances. I really wanted for us to have privacy, jobs, financial security and romance but we were stuck living with his dad and there was no resolution or forward movement in sight.

I soon found myself comparing our relationship to others around me and it made my marriage feel like a hopeless big black hole. Social media is a great way to connect with friends and family but when we are not careful can be a dangerous place. While I was trapped in my unfulfilling marriage, feeling a huge lack of love and attention, people were posting pictures of huge engagement rings, big romantic weddings, the keys to their new house, babies on the way, fun and happy date nights, quick getaways, special surprises and how much they loved being with their "best friends" (just gag me already!) All I had to do was log onto my social media accounts to see all the things I really wanted and was never going to have with this man.

Since communication has always been important to me, I did not hesitate to express my dissatisfaction to him. I thought that telling it like it was would motivate him to correct the issue. *Honesty is the best policy, right?* I called him names, belittled him, and tore him to shreds with my words. I over-shared with friends some of the things that he was doing wrong. I spent a lot of time on the phone with my sister-in-law that first year telling her all the things her brother was doing wrong. I admired her faith, her family and her relationship and I hoped that there was something she could say or do to make things better for us. After almost 10 months of total unmanageable craziness, she finally told me, "Tiffany, you guys need to see a professional counselor. I cannot help you."

GETTING HELP

I thought that seeing a counselor was accepting defeat and by doing so would be the beginning of the end for us. She would see how selfish and unreasonable he was and how I deserved so much more for myself. We could get an outside opinion from an uninvolved party about how acceptable divorce would be under this very special and unique circumstance. So we went and I had no problem speaking up first. I wanted her to know that I was better than this crazy chaos. I was a college graduate of sound mind and not altered by any substances, unlike my husband. He was doing everything wrong and if *he* doesn't change I am out of here! It didn't take long before she started calling me out on my wrongs. In the sessions some light was shed on my manipulative, hurtful and disrespectful behavior and language. Even though I was feeling resentful, angry, insecure and sad, it was not okay to treat my husband this way. *She had some nerve I tell you!*

Our marriage seemed to go from bad to worse in the couple of months between starting counseling and celebrating our one year anniversary. He still wasn't working, we were living with his dad, there was no resolution in sight and he started drinking again. From all the horrible things that had happened when he drank before I could only imagine where this was going to lead. Some nights he would pick up some beer and drink it at home. Some nights he would go out and drink with the boys. Some nights his friends would leave him on the side of the road and some nights he didn't come home at all. That first morning I woke up alone, my first thought was, "he better be dead!" In my frustration and rage, bricks of bitterness, anger, hurt and resentment were added to the protective wall I was building around my heart. I didn't understand the disease of alcoholism and how it is a progressive disease. I did not know then that it only gets worse never better.

Shortly after Ryan started drinking again the counselor advised me to attend a 12 step program to learn about the disease of alcoholism. It didn't make sense to me. Since I didn't have the drinking problem *why was she advising me to seek help and not him? He was the one with the problem that needed fixing!* But being the good student I am, I made sure to do my homework and attend one meeting before our next session. I went with the idea in mind that I would discover ways to help my husband get sober... Or justification to leave him... The first meeting I attended I heard the following:

- Attend at least 6 meetings before deciding if this is for me
- Don't be a doormat
- Don't make threats you don't intend to carry out
- Do play, have fun and find recreation

I knew that nobody in those rooms could help me because we had nothing in common. My circumstance was hopeless. I heard from people whose qualifiers were sober and people whose qualifiers were still out on benders. But since my story really hadn't even been written yet I didn't hear my story the way I needed to hear it. I opened my mouth to share and all I could do was cry. It was hopeless, my sister-in-law couldn't help me, my counselor couldn't help me and these people certainly were not going to be able to help me. *How did I get here anyways!?*

After attending a few meetings, I discovered that the people in these rooms actually had something that I wanted. In the crazy and the chaos they found ways to cope and find peace and serenity and Lord knows I needed more of that. I continued to attend the meetings. I had a safe place to share my struggles with people who could relate and wouldn't judge me or my marriage. After a little time in the program, I think I may have even been a little more pleasant to be around when I saw my friends.

THE LAST STRAW

After several months of us both not working I found a decent job and Ryan decided to start his own business. There were some start up costs which we discussed and justified together. He needed a special program in order to do his 3-D design and he got a laptop so he could work remotely. That was all fine until he discovered that there was a bigger and better laptop that came out and he had to have it. He bought a second laptop spending in total what would could have been at least seven months' rent in Southern California. All that, while we were living with his dad because we could not afford to live on our own. I was livid! At that point I was feeling stuck. This went against my plan and everything I was trying to accomplish getting out of debt, saving money, buying a house and starting our family. It was one of my "last straw" moments.

I was getting ready for our annual canoeing trip and I expected the truck to be loaded up and ready to go by the time I got home from work. Instead, I was greeted by an inebriated husband, who was not ready. We still had to pick up two friends on the way and after a long day's work, I was now left to load the truck by myself and drive. I was infuriated, I would have left without him, but I didn't want to have to explain to my friends where my husband was and why we didn't come together. When we pulled out of the driveway, I was tearing down the street like a madwoman. Ryan told me, "slow down you are going to kill somebody!"

To which I responded "I would rather us both die than live with you!" This was an eye opening moment for me since, as a general rule, I have never been one to wish anyone else (or myself) dead. After I calmed myself down enough we safely made it to the river and we had a good weekend when we got there.

We had a counseling session when we got back. When he didn't show up, that was the straw that broke the camel's back for me. I still had the truck from our camping trip and I told the counselor that I was loading that truck up and leaving Ryan. I didn't think I was serious till she called me on my bluff and started to support the idea. This was not a new statement I had made and she was familiar with the program principal, "don't make threats you don't intend to carry out," so she helped me process this decision. We walked through how I was going to tell him and how he would feel and react. Luckily I had family close by that I could humble myself enough to run to, but it didn't come without the feeling of shame and a serious blow to my pride. My image and dignity (if I had any left) was definitely tarnished.

After about 15 months of marriage we started a physical separation. At the time I had a very long list of everything that led me to make that decision and an even longer list of "Mandatory Accomplishments Before I Take You Back". At the rate we were going, I put a six month expiration date on our marriage and I was not hopeful that we were going to make it. I moved in with my sweet grandma. I spent time working, started training for a marathon and actually started to pray harder to God. I asked for a miracle for my marriage and for a clear cut answer as to which direction I should take, whether it be to stay or go. I hated the feeling of limbo and not knowing. I just want to know which direction to take at this fork in the road!

TOTAL DEVASTATION

We had been physically separated for about two months when God answered my prayer for a clear cut answer. It is true what they say, "be careful what you wish for". It was four o'clock in the morning, just a few days before Christmas, when I was awakened by a phone call. By the time I answered, he was a drunken, sobbing, blubbering mess. He was telling me that he was sorry, that our marriage was over, that I was never going to forgive him and that he needed to see me right now. In that moment I felt sad for him, sad for me. Suspecting what had happened I felt angry and sick to my stomach. Hearing him tell me that our marriage was over left me feeling rejected and devastated. He came over at that ungodly hour to tell me about the mistake he had made with another woman in an altered state. He had just left there, he was sorry and had to tell me right away. Sleep deprivation combined with shock, hurt and total devastation, I dismissed him. I had nothing to say. I was trembling and my teeth were chattering. It was the wee hours on a December morning so I was probably a little cold but mostly it was my over-stimulated nerves. I removed my wedding ring immediately as I was sure this was the clear sign from God I had been asking for. There would be no way to recover from this.

That Christmas I was embarrassed, ashamed and broken down. The "protective barrier" around my heart received a few more bricks of hurt, resentment and anger. With all the uncertainty life had thrown my way I avoided my family; I just couldn't cope. I didn't want to answer any questions, I didn't want to see anyone who might judge me or try to offer useless advice. I was humiliated and had lost all dignity. I was sure nobody else had ever felt this much pain, anger and uncertainty. *Yes marriage is hard but nobody has ever had it as hard as I do right now.* I was able to decorate a little tree very late on Christmas Eve to make it special for my grandma but other than that Christmas was cancelled for Tiffany.

Ryan started to reach out to me the way I had always longed for. He would call me daily and leave me sweet updates and messages about how he was doing. He would invite me out for coffee to get fresh air and try to get me out of my depressed funk. He sent flowers. In those moments, I felt loved, appreciated and cared for the way I had longed to feel. He shared that he was making new friends and attending a 12 step program, all that it was doing for him and all the miracles that families had experienced in the program in the past. But for me, it was too little too late. I was not going to wait anymore to see how much worse it could get for us. *How long would he stay sober this time? Bring me the divorce papers already. I AM DONE!*

TURNING POINT

A couple weeks after Christmas I got a call from my uncle. I didn't want to talk, I just wanted to be left alone. I was afraid he would ask questions, *why did I miss Christmas? What are you going to do? Of all questions, please don't ask me how I am doing!* Despite my apprehensions, I picked up the phone and I am so glad I did. That God-loving man shared his marriage testimony with me and it was absolutely shocking. He fearlessly and courageously opened up to me about some of the struggles he had experienced in his marriage and how, over time, he saw a transformation in his wife's heart. It was a long healing process but he saw strength, humility, light, love, grace and Christ-like forgiveness and it had changed him and the fate of his marriage and family. During that conversation I had recalled a few years prior, during Thanksgiving, him giving thanks for his wife and all the hardships that they had endured. At the time, I thought *how hard could the hardships really be in such a perfect relationship?* I am so thankful for my uncle and his transparency. In his moments of unveiled honesty I became open to the idea of a different outcome for our story.

I continued to pray. I prayed for peace for myself, I prayed for my husband's sobriety, I prayed for my marriage and my sanity. I prayed for wisdom and guidance. I prayed for God's will and then contradicted it with "please give us immediate resolution," which, as we know, only comes in God's perfect timing. In despair, many of us put that "rush" stamp on our prayers, I know I did. I also continued attending my support group which was such a blessing to help cope and process all that was going on without having to process it with friends who wouldn't understand why I was sticking around. I worked with a sponsor and did a "fearless and searching moral inventory," looking at the nature of my wrongs, which empowered me by removing "victim" and "martyr" as labels for myself. I also gathered a few more pointers to live by:

- Don't give up before the miracle happens
- Get out of God's way and let His will be done
- Stop trying to be God
- Focus on what you CAN change and that is yourself

After living with my grandma for about 10 months I moved into a darling little 345 square foot studio backhouse. My husband was starting to take the steps I had hoped he would in order for us to be together but was not yet meeting my expectations. It was going to take time to heal the pain. It was going to take even more time to build up the trust again. Part of me wanted to leave him and have a fresh start, but the selfish part of me held on out of fear that this would be the change he needed to become the man I always knew he could be. *I'll be darned if another woman would reap the benefits of all my effort and patience.* We did things separately and together and we enjoyed each other in the privacy of my little studio. I started to feel more pride and dignity than I had in years. I finally had a little independence and felt a huge sense of accomplishment when I crossed the finish line of my first full marathon. It was nice to focus on something good for myself rather than the chaos and disappointments.

As time went on, the pain and uncertainty eased up. We dated each other and living separately made it kind of fun. He got to pick me up and drop me off (or spend the night). I still struggled with wanting to know how it was supposed to be (patience has never been one of my strong suits).

NEW BEGINNINGS

We had been living separately for about 17 months when we found out we were expecting a baby. We were surprised to say the least. Ryan had not yet met all the criteria on my list of "Mandatory Accomplishments Before I Take You Back". Whether or not we stayed together, one thing was for sure, we would always be a part of each others' life now. Ryan got a job with one of the clients he had been working with and had been sober for just over a year with the help of a 12 step program. I continued to pray for God's will and guidance. We waited till I was five months along before we finally agreed that our period of separation should come to an end. With a baby on the way I welcomed my husband with his toothbrush, clothes and his computer making, us a complete family. By the time we celebrated our three year wedding anniversary we had been separated for almost two years.

We welcomed our baby boy on December 5th, 2010. He was the best surprise and miracle I ever could have asked for. He was everything I had ever dreamed of and more. All the lyrics to all those sappy love songs finally made sense to me, especially Aerosmith's *Don't Want to Miss a Thing*. He brought us so much joy I was over the moon. I was getting closer to having all I had ever wanted but God still had His work cut out for Himself with me. Overtime, I had built a seemingly indestructible wall around my heart. It housed, bitterness, anger and resentment. I was still obsessive and controlling and much like our newlywed days, my husband couldn't do anything right. *Give him a bottle, don't give him a bottle (I need to nurse). Change his diaper. Don't change his diaper (we don't want to waste them!) Spend time with him, hold him, read him a book! Why aren't you helping me!?* I would blame the hormones but who am I kidding? I was nuts. The same sharp tongue I had as a new wife came back with fangs!

I called my friend to tell her I wanted to celebrate myself for the upcoming Father's Day, instead of Ryan. She spoke up and reminded me that a father has a very important role in a child's life and that God intended for children to have a father and a mother. She reminded me that man and wife are two separate and different people and God created us that way. A child needs his father just as much as he needs his mother. She reminded me that I needed to respect that. I want to tell you that I doted on her every word in that very moment, but I was too angry and rebellious. It took me a couple of years after that conversation to come back to her and say, "you were right. Thank you so much for speaking light, love, truth and wisdom instead of just telling me what I wanted to hear!"

We saw our marriage counselor for about eight months in our early years of marriage. We stopped going after that dreadful December incident since our marriage was through. After our son turned one we decided to go back to her and we frequented her couch for about two years the second time around. We dug deep and some sessions were playful, some were painful but I have to say it has been one of the best investments of time and money we could have made in our marriage. Despite the initial feelings of shame that came with having to accept that we needed the help, I can't say enough about how amazing marriage counseling can be even for those who are not "in trouble". We have learned so much about ourselves and how our childhoods shaped who we are today. We learned more about each other in those sessions than we ever would have thought to learn on our own. I didn't appreciate hearing that I was manipulative, condescending, and disrespectful but if I had ignored those facts and decided to leave Ryan, I would have dragged that destructive behavior into a second marriage, maybe even a third. I am so beyond thankful that Ryan was willing to go to counseling. It takes a real man to step up and be willing, open and receptive to an outside opinion and expertise.

Another ground breaking fact that I had to understand was the importance of respecting my husband. One of the many differences between men and women is that women have a need to be loved, desired and pursued and men have a deep need to be respected. It took a lot of soul searching to realize that even when I didn't think my husband deserved respect, I was commanded by God to honor and respect him. Honestly I am still a work in progress in this department, but here are a few guidelines I try to use to respect my husband no matter what:

- Give him the dignity to do things his way (even if I feel there is a better way)
- Talk positively about him
- Encourage him
- Praise him
- Never talk bad about your husband EVER

I could write a whole book on this topic alone (many are already on the shelves!) so I will share from *Ephesians 5:33 "Each one of you must love his wife as he loves himself and the wife must respect her husband."*

Shortly after we were blessed with our second son, I had an epiphany. Someday my precious baby boys are going to find a woman to marry. Since they are human I can predict with 101% certainty, even if Ryan and I do everything right, they will mess up, they will say and do things they shouldn't say and they will likely drop the ball occasionally. My heart aches at the thought of a woman treating my baby boys the way that I have treated my husband. If I could take it all back, I would. The words I spoke were a reflection of the ugliness in my heart and not of my husband. It is my prayer that I show my boys what a kind, loving, gentle wife looks like so that they make a wise decision when choosing a wife some day.

In case we are not yet convinced that my language and behavior was unacceptable, the book of Proverbs has several verses describing a "quarrelsome wife" and basically liken me to the "dripping of a leaky roof in a rainstorm;" restraining me is like "restraining the wind or grasping oil with the hand" *(Proverbs 27:15-16).* Ryan would have been "better off living alone in the desert" (Proverbs 21:19) or "on the corner of a leaky roof" (Proverbs 25:24) than with me. If that doesn't prove I was out of control, I don't know what does.

While having goals and hopes for the future are necessary to succeed, I realize how unrealistic my expectations were for Ryan. I was seeking from him what only God can provide. No flesh and blood or worldly materials can meet my expectations since there is no "enough" gage on my expectation meter. I have a void that is meant to be filled with the Holy Spirit only and I was running on empty for a long time. It wasn't pretty. Ryan's race to my finish line was more like a labyrinth with ever changing dead ends and detours. He was chasing after a finish line that doesn't even exist. Instead of teaming up with him, I treated him like an enemy compromising God's perfect design for our marriage.

KNOCKING THE WALLS DOWN

Over time I had unintentionally built a wall around my heart. It started from my childhood experiences, but that is a whole other story. The bricks I used to build the protective wall consisted of anger, bitterness and resentment. Just like Eve hid from God in the Garden of Eden as she was aware she was naked (Gen 3:8), I tried to hide behind the wall that housed my insecurities, expectations, pride, and all the things I didn't want to let go of and give to God. It was supposed to prevent me from having to be vulnerable and was intended to protect me from pain and disappointment but our all-knowing God could see right through it and we all know how well that worked out for me.

In April of 2014 I hit my rock bottom. My husband had been sober for over five years, he was treating me well, we had two perfect healthy boys who brought me more joy than I ever imagined possible, I was blessed with the opportunity to be home with my babies just like I wanted. Everything on the outside was actually really good for us but I still felt toxic on the inside letting fear, anxiety, and resentment contribute to what would be my demise if something didn't change. I was living in my own personal hell. I could no longer blame my husband or anyone else for unmet expectations, and I was forced to turn around and look in the mirror. The glimpse I caught of myself was painful and I couldn't handle the feelings of anger, resentment and bitterness anymore. I sat down in tears and wrote a bold prayer asking God to search my heart and replace my toxic feelings with peace, love and tenderness. I also asked Him to turn my story into a testimony (having no idea that my best friend would ask me to publish it almost a year after this prayer).

Almost immediately following my bold prayer, I started experiencing gratitude on a whole new level. In the same notebook I wrote that prayer, I made a gratitude list and praised God even while I was still in my storm. After I started letting Him knock the walls down to reveal and heal my heart, I started to experience a taste of freedom. This verse from Philippians actually resonated with me:

Do not be anxious about anything, but in everything by prayer and supplication with thanksgiving let your requests be made known to God. And the peace of God, which surpasses all understanding, will guard your hearts and your minds in Christ Jesus. (Phil 4:6-7)

I can't tell you how many times I have been advised and encouraged to make a gratitude list. Some days are easier than others but when I actually do, my negative feelings actually ease up if not go away completely. I have had to learn to praise God in the storm. Here is one of my favorite verses on that:

Romans 5:3 -5 We rejoice in our sufferings, knowing that suffering produces endurance, and endurance produces character, and character produces hope, and hope does not put us to shame, because God's love has been poured into our hearts through the Holy Spirit who has been given to us.

RESTORATION

Looking back now I can only imagine God shaking his head at me saying, "Tiffany, O ye of little faith!" Our story didn't unfold nearly as I had planned. God orchestrated it better than I could have ever hoped. It has been a roller coaster filled with tears, more tears, miracles, laughter, disagreements, love, joy, faithfulness and hope. Ryan has been sober and active in his program for over 6 years. We just celebrated our 8th wedding anniversary. We now have two sweet and spunky boys; Drew is four and Blake is two. I get to be a work-at-home-mom, Ryan takes the train to work and after several moves this past year God answered my prayers and opened the doors to our first home. Aside from our mortgage, we live a debt free life.

Ryan is not the same "boy" I met when I was seventeen, I am not the same "girl" either. We have grown both together and separately and we are still a work in progress. We are learning to embrace the seasons, adapt as the times change and most importantly enjoy each other. We still disagree and have heated arguments. We are two sinners joined together and bound to disappoint each other whether we want to or not. Some days we have to work harder than others, but we have more good days than not. He still makes me laugh like no one else can and he makes me feel like a smitten little school girl when he wants to. He knows me better than I know myself sometimes. I love our inside jokes, bedtime giggles and the things that are only funny because we know each other so well. I have found a beautiful friend in my husband and I can't believe it took me so long to realize what an amazing gift he is to me.

To answer my mom's question, Ryan is a wonderful father. I absolutely love the way he plays with our boys and makes them laugh. They adore their daddy and can always count on him being the "fun one". They want to grow up to be big and strong just like him. He takes such good care of us all and I can't imagine having a family with any other man. Oh, and I was right, he makes beautiful babies!

INTO THE SUNSET

Seven years ago this story was aired out dirty laundry. It has been through the wash and pressed a few times and I am both humbled and terrified for the opportunity to share my marriage testimony. It is my hope and prayer that it helps at least one other person through a challenging time whether they relate to every little detail or some of the underlying concepts and feelings. I am so glad I didn't give up before our miracle. One of the coolest parts about our story is that it is only just beginning. God is still writing His story with us as we speak. While there are likely some storms on the horizon, such is life, I believe the best is yet to come.

Kaleidoscope
Coping with Changes

Life can be completely unpredictable. As a child one of my favorite toys was a kaleidoscope. I loved looking at the pretty colors and with every turn the image would change, never to return to a previous image. We can fight it, but no matter how many times we turn the kaleidoscope it will never be the same and our only option is to get used to the new view. In life we can plan for our future and we can set goals to work towards but like the kaleidoscope things can change indefinitely. Tiffany desired a change in her life and it came in the form of her heart. Sometimes change is undesired and the transformation comes in learning to deal with it. Change happens. Bad things happen. Our lives are sometimes for a moment unpredictable and out of our control. We have talked about options with coping with new circumstances but sometimes your only option is to move on the best you can. We will lose some battles, but that doesn't mean we will lose the war. The Band Rise Against has lyrics that say, "How you survive is what makes you who you are." How we choose to move on from a situation will help build our character and mold our future.

Kimberly is a woman who let love transform her life. Similar to Tiffany she had her mind set on the way things should be but when the sudden twist of the kaleidoscope brought tragedy into her life she had to pick up the pieces and learn to live with loss.

Kimberly Timpe

IN THE BEGINNING

I started out my life journey feeling like I was an unbreakable girl. I felt like a rock so grounded and unaffected by dangers and random chaos that had affected so many others. I was a girl who had not lost anyone to death. I felt immortal, untouchable and even superhuman. Death and sickness were things that only happened to other people, or to old people, not to those in my life. Loss was something that never crossed my mind. I was ignorant.

Growing up, I didn't want to get married or have children. I craved a life of art, travel and unrestricted freedom, allowing me to wander into my own happiness. My plans changed drastically in December of 2002 when I met the man who would change my world. The day was crisp and the evening's darkness became imminent. I held onto every second I could till I had to run home before it was pitch black out. The kisses were intense and deep and we had an instant chemical attraction. I wanted to be with him more than anything I originally thought I wanted out of life. Going to school to be a human rights attorney practically fell off of my "to do" list. My studies weren't as important to me as the time that could be spent with him. After our meeting, my desires changed, I became a codependent person.

I wanted to be where he was and to do the things he did. I wanted to wrap my soul around his and keep him close without clipping his wings of individual freedom. We were inseparable after that cool December day; he was picking me up after school and cheer practice and we spent every day together. Our connection was more than physical and chemical. There was a familiar understanding between us. He knew what I liked and wanted without me having to express myself. He was thoughtful and intriguing. I had never met someone who could keep me on my toes like he did. I needed to keep him; we belonged together with each other from the very start.

Eventually my parents invited him to stay in our motor home because he was sleeping in his truck out front of my house just waiting for a new day that we could spend together. I knew it in my heart that this was the man I was going grow old with. We day dreamed and talked about raising our children and watching our grandchildren play while we sat on our front porch swing. We were so certain of what our old wrinkly selves were going to be up to! Everyday life became mundane when we were apart and those things that kept us apart were the enemy to which we needed to rebel and break free from. Our perceptions of life were twisted a year or so later, in which those mundane bumps, or responsibilities, became issues in our union. While our reactions to these situations were in our control we did not take responsibility for them. Noticing the changes that had taken place in our relationship, I began trying to clip his wings and tame him despite my original intentions of keeping him free. I wanted to manipulate and control, never quite grasping how to love him and in turn forgetting how to love myself. All of my emotions and activities were determined by our daily relationship.

GROWNUPS

Sam and I always knew we were going to get married, no matter how bad the fights, or how bad the situation; we were made for each other. In 2008 he was selected to perform duties for the U.S. Army and he asked me to marry him before he was deployed. I was much obliged and soon after became pregnant. Neither one of us particularly cared to have a wedding but we went to the courthouse and planned to do a celebration upon his return from Afghanistan. I found it so fulfilling and fun to think of sharing events over that year with my pregnancy and new baby and him doing this admirable deed for our nation; what more could we celebrate!? It just seemed right to combine and recognize all of our joint accomplishments.

The pregnancy and deployment times in our lives were very strange for me. I was living with my parents thinking about this wonderful thing happening inside me, my mind wrapped in heavenly thoughts about my baby and future. Meanwhile, I was constrained with guilt over the deployment and locality of my husband. Hour to hour truly felt like he was 7,400 miles away. There were some weeks without any communication with him and when there was opportunity to connect, I worked on being upbeat because he was clearly down. It was obvious the war had weighed heavy on his heart and those things were not appropriate to talk about over the phone. Our connection was shaky and it wasn't always the phone line's fault. I feel many of his experiences turned into stone gargoyles cast into his memory bank saved for the nightmares when he returned home to my heaven.

As my belly grew so did the anticipation of his return. I worried everyday about him and if the care packages I sent were going to make him happy or sustain any sense of normalcy at all. I was clueless about real PTSD (post-traumatic stress syndrome) and how I could have been a better partner for him. I'm not really sure that reading all the books in the world could have prepared me for the issues that followed his return from war.

Sammy wasn't the same person when he returned from Afghanistan. On the inside he was altered in a troubling way and I believe haunted by those very experiences that seasoned his soul. He didn't want to talk about the war, nor did he accept any help. The reflection of me that I once saw in him had tarnished. It seems he grew sadder over that year as I grew more fulfilled. I felt he had a hard time adjusting to sharing me with this new baby. On top of all that, he never got to bond with her at birth like most fathers since she was eight months old by the time he returned. I was trying to make it work. Our daughter, Chanel had colic and cried a lot which triggered more anxiety in him. Because I was a stay at home mom during her first year and I was her primary caregiver, Chanel looked to me for comfort. Anxiety prohibited the effort that he needed to fully develop their father/daughter bond. Not only that, spending time to bond and form a connection with her was not on his agenda. I didn't understand why there was rain on my parade. I was exhausting the three of us by trying to force him to take initiative as a father. This is when things got rough on an intimate level for our little family. It was easier for him to go have fun without us and was easier to pass the responsibilities onto me; but I wanted them anyway, ***my way***. The things Sam and I always did together were no longer fun with a whinny baby and nagging wife.

INTO THE DARKNESS

The dark moments were mean. We were mean; both filled with jealousy and resentment. That man could make my blood boil! My love for him was suppressed so deep down in my heart that even in the reddest of faces and clenched fists, all I wanted was for everything to be better than it was before the fight. We parted ways and got back together over and over. It was a toxic relationship with highly addictive qualities. Ultimately, it wasn't the life we wanted and we knew our daughter deserved parents who were as happy as we could possibly be. Our happiness was overshadowed by the fact that neither of us wanted to be controlled and we never stopped trying to control each other.

Eventually, I had enough. Chanel and I moved to my parents' home and I worked hard to get back on my feet while still trying to maintain the majority of time with my daughter. My parents were a tremendous help and so were his. I knew that if I ever needed anything, I had those four there for support, so I never felt alone, aside from the heartbreak of not understanding why he wouldn't communicate and work harder to keep us.

I started and dominated the custody and divorce paper work. I had some prior experience because of my career path; I had a paralegal certification and possessed a determined mother-hen mindset. Our daughter was going to be cared for under my rules. He didn't like that. It was a constant struggle for him to get visitation, but then he wouldn't show up, or he wouldn't follow the rules. I felt like I had done all of the work all her life and he was a threat to ruin it or take it away from me.

This was one of the most trying situations of my life. I wanted my daughter to be with her father but I wanted her father to want to be with his daughter in an appropriate setting. It didn't feel like too much to ask but the dialogue in my mind played on and on, *"perhaps I'm asking too much, perhaps my rules are too hard for him to follow, maybe I should allow him to take her here or there, even though I know they are irresponsible people and in party atmospheres."*

A sharp "no" often quickly escaped from my mouth when he asked to take her places. The war had moved from Afghanistan to our home front, but he knew a battle, with me, wasn't one he would win. I love her far too much to overlook the environment, influence or small stuff that would threaten the work I had done in raising her. The battle raged inside my heart as well as in our relationship. I just wanted to raise a happy, healthy, and trauma-free daughter.

When it came to her, I held everything against him. He made it quite easy; however, bringing new women into the situation, splurging on trips and booze instead of using the money for child support. My heart was now full of anger and resentment. I thought, *"YOU wanted this child, I never wanted to get married or have this life."* These were things I often said to him and myself, angry that my life had been changed so much; I felt he owed me for taking away my individual freedom. I felt defeated and tied down to this man who wanted to keep me but had no intentions of sharing the responsibilities of our daughter. Ball and chains bound us in this serious custody situation.

I held onto the anger of his lack of parental responsibilities and I reminded him every chance I got. I put him down and he put me down. He blamed me and I blamed him. A vicious, constant tug of war was happening between us.

Sam and I had gone in and out of our relationship, never quite letting go. He had his cake and ate it too. I still felt like we were best friends and that it was still he and I against the world. This went on for 12 years, back and forth, love and hate, the balance was never tangible like our seemingly ill-fated connection. I longed for something different. He had openly dated other women and I understood we needed to move on. Our sceneries changed; I got a house, he moved six hundred miles away from northern CA to southern CA and did border patrol for the Army. Chanel and I often visited him for family vacations where our time together was oddly a perfect balance of being disconnectedly connected.

ACCEPTING NEW CHANGES

I am certain we had always planned we could get back together eventually even if it was decades later. I thought it was good that he dated others even if I didn't date so much because I rationalized that we would appreciate each other more when we reunited. In December of 2012 I met the man who would become my second boyfriend ever. I had never committed to telling Sam goodbye for good because any other guy who came into my life was more like a pawn to show him how it felt to be pushed aside for another. This attitude was a bit of a "tit for tat." This new guy was different; I had fun with him and he was smart and had things going for himself. Sam didn't like that I had seemingly moved on. I remember asking him, "I've never asked you not to interfere with my love life before, but this time, I'm begging you to let me move on because you're not going to change anytime soon."

Deep down I knew that Sam was still the person I wanted to sit with on the front porch swing in old age (I fantasized he would build the swing with his own hands). My hope of him coming around and settling down never changed. I never had that love with anyone else and I don't plan to ever find a connection as intense. I am fine with this realization because what we had in those good times are incomparable to any other.

During the first six months of my new relationship, Sam would reach out to me. Sometimes he would reach out with complimentary or random things; other times he was angry. Often times he wanted to continue conversations that exceeded the dialog of the visitation schedules. He felt that this new man of mine infringed on what had always been his. I was committed to trying something new with someone new and all the drama and small talk in the world was not going to rip me away from an opportunity to grow- even if it was with someone new.

I experienced much growth indeed! I learned that relationships deserve compromise and flexibility. Besides, Sam appeared to be quite successful playing the field; he was seemingly getting his life in order as well. For the first time in years he had his own place and was hanging out with his roommate, Chris, a guy who appeared to be a good influence. Chris had a lot in common with Sam. He seemed to encourage Sam into more responsible habits. As Sam's confidence grew, he became more interested in spending time with our daughter. He seemed to be settling into the later years of his twenties with a hopeful outlook about his abilities as a man. I also experienced a newfound confidence with my new partner; I was refreshed, and I felt discovered again, as a woman, as a person.

I was really happy and relieved that Samuel seemed to be stepping up to his obligations as a civilian back in society. I was happier that he thought of his daughter in those times of prosperity. Although, I was still not comfortable with her going to his home without supervision, even if his roommate had three kids for her to interact with there. His rent was paid, the house was clean, and other mothers let their children visit, but I did not. My instinct said the distance was too far for me to feel comfortable even though he reassured me she would be provided with the upmost care. Another hard "no" came from my mouth. I was conflicted about the restrictions I gave him because I felt that he was growing in so many ways. I felt his "tiger stripes" had indeed matured, but they were not any different than before even though I was hopeful for more progress.

DEVASTATION

On June 27th 2013 my world dramatically changed without warning. I remember the day that my heart broke; it is forever etched in my memory. I was driving my daughter to a doctor's appointment when I got a call from a mutual friend named Schelley. "Hey!" she said, "how are you doing?"

"Good," I replied, "just off to do some errands! You?"

She began with, "So, I'm assuming you haven't heard about Sam?"

"Oh God, now what?" I glibly asked as a reference to past heart breaks inflicted by him. I suspected he was having some legal issue or did some ridiculous stunt that would break his streak of good behavior.

"Well, I want you to pull your car over before I tell you," she instructed. With my daughter sleeping in the back of the car, I pulled over. "Sam got into a fight last night, Kimmie, he didn't make it, and I'm so sorry honey."

I had never been so grateful for the soothing motion of the car that lulled my sweet baby to sleep that day. In that moment, time froze. I didn't believe her. I told her, "No way, I'm going to call him right now and he will answer."

There I sat, on the side of the road making call after call to him, countless times, to get no answer. Nothing. I was in disbelief. I was in total shock. Sam was invincible in my eyes. I thought, *"How could this have happened? Sam had a fight; with who?"* Schelley said that it was Chris. Through the confusion I thought, *"The guy Sam was living with who was helping to get him on his feet? The same friend who was also a military man? The same man who came to my house a week earlier with several boxes of hand-me-down clothes from his daughters because he said he felt bad that I had no help from him? The same man who drove him to the unemployment office and alerted me that he got him to sign up and informed me I should check my account to ensure they pulled child support from his check? This same guy who had degrees, an ex-wife, a couple of kids, a home, and an extra truck for my husband to borrow so he could better himself?"* This man, Chris, turned out to be the monster who murdered my husband, my love, my greatest teacher. This is the man who seemed like a true friend there to help his buddy up and out of a tough situation. This didn't make sense to me and couldn't be true. I didn't understand.

I was unable to comprehend the information I was told, so I called Sam's mom and dad, "Hi, did you guys hear anything crazy?" I asked Sam's stepmother Sharon.

"Yes, Kimmie, it's true. We're on our way to your house now," she replied.

On the corner of a bustling intersection in my little town, I experienced a total emotional and mental collapse. My head shook and I trembled and even with the erratic physical movement, I felt nothingness; nothing at all. I was in shock. Tears began to stream like waterfalls down my face. While part of my world slept in the back seat of the car, I realized that the other part of my world was gone.

We skipped the doctor's appointment and arrived home to many teary eyed people. I held myself together as best as I could for Sam's mother and father. Sam's father had spent his morning at the crime scene trying to get some answers. I couldn't imagine how he felt that his child was violently stolen from him.

After the house cleared of grieving people, Chanel found me collapsed and crying on my bedroom floor. She'd never witnessed this behavior from her mother before in her four years of life. I'd always kept it together for her sake. Chanel didn't understand the sudden crowd in the house, but she sensed it was not normal for mommy to be a soggy mess on the floor. She knelt down in front of me, placed her hands on my shoulders and said, "Mommy, why are you so sad?" I didn't know what to say. Telling my baby that her father was dead was something I never planned to say.

"I'm sad because we can't ever see your daddy again, no one can, and he's gone forever," I cried.

She told me she would be right back and returned with a posse of stuffed animals to which she organized in a big circle around me on the floor. When she was done, she gave me a big hug and said, "I'm here, mommy, you have me."

This beautiful soul knew just what to say to make me feel strong again. She encouraged me to get back up on my feet and parent like I'd never done before, not only for her, but also for him, because he would never know the healing love in that hug. She filled a huge hole in my soul with pure love, innocence, and purpose.

The life ending trauma Sam endured was horrific. He died from multiple stab wounds which started in the garage, traveled through Chris' home, where his children and girlfriend apparently were. Evidence suggested Sam tried to run from Chris yelling for help as he ran around a neighbor's parked car. He was successful in getting the attention of the neighbor across the street who called 911. The call was placed with urgency, but the neighbor thought Chris' intention was to give aid to Sam. It was too late to save Sam from his fate where he was finished off with a slit of the throat on the neighbor's doorstep.

Chris was apprehended immediately after the incident. Sam's dad spent the early morning hours trying to gather information to make any sense of the situation. But there was none. It was a senseless act. Our family shared the loss and confusion together, binding us in a morbid way which I believe has given each of us a deeper appreciation and thirst for life.

Many rumors circulated about Chris' motive for killing Sam. Each speculation left us more empty and confused. The plot thickened two weeks after Sam's passing when Chris' girlfriend (who was present during the murder) committed suicide. Another life was tragically gone. More questions ensued. The incident was difficult to comprehend. It still is. The entire situation was twisted with "maybe's" and "what-if's". We don't know what events led up to the murder that night or how something could go so terribly wrong.

PICKING UP THE PIECES

The weeks and months following Sam's death were filled

with friends, family, and condolences to which I had no response. Media coverage was an issue for us; the news, the papers, everyone wanted the story. They wanted to know the details of what happened. Sam's dad made it clear that he didn't want attention focused on the manner in which he passed, but rather the things he accomplished in life. The media couldn't get the story right anyway. Along with media came detectives. I had several calls coming in each day and weeks following the event. I had been separated from Sam for nearly six months before the incident. I had no information to offer and declined all interviews; ironically, I felt guilt in my low moments. The fact that I was so dedicated, loving and committed to Sam for 12 years of his life, only to let go of the last six months of his existence made me feel extremely guilty. Words can't express my guilt for not hanging in there and I am sad for letting him see that I had eventually moved on during the last days of his life.

I felt frustration and anxiety over the anticipation of events that followed Sam's death. I just wanted the funeral to be over. I couldn't bare thinking of the body that I once worshipped contained in a small box being put into the ground. The beautiful service was fit for a veteran and the place was packed with mourners. The cemetery was gorgeous. That night, there was an intimate gathering of his friends and it was unnatural for me to be there without him, so my mind pictured him off laughing somewhere out of my sight.

A year after Sam's passing, the murder trial finally happened and it was the fastest case our advocates had ever seen at Tehama County Courts. It was a few days long and Chris was found guilty of first degree murder and was sentenced to life in prison. Unfortunately, our family gained no insight into the reason for such a horrid violation on our loved one. The justice system need only prove that the crime was committed.

This experience has opened me up to my awareness of being. Life is a delicate balance, a dance we all live by and I am making it a point to do it gracefully because life is very fragile; so fragile that it is out of our control. Death has become an invisible man who stalks and threatens to take any life, at any time, and I am aware of his presence now.

REMEMBERING SAM

At times, I can feel Sam's hands on my shoulders guiding me to have more fun, to let loose, or tell Chanel "no" to things that I don't think he would appreciate. His influence encourages not only her, but me to do things that we are afraid of, because he would. Everyday his intentions are in my parenting. He is with us. During the times I want to share with him I realize that he is the deep inhalation of air that I breathe. He's the vibration from the beat of our favorite songs. He's the shifty smile on my daughter's face when she's really interested in something. He's not with us physically anymore, but I feel his presence.

Sometimes, knowingly, victims are victims of choice. Some want to be loved for the wounds they have lived through and be recognized for the scabs and scars that remain. Not me; I want to love and be loved for the things about to come; for the future moments that will enrich each next chapter with more wisdom than the next. To rehash the wounds is for the birds. I consider my future. What can I do every day to make sure I am contributing to a better tomorrow? I feel great about even the smallest of feats like paying a bill, or following up on a call on those days where I don't want to leave the shrine that I call my bed. I pat myself on my back for doing the most miniscule of tasks like that, because life is tough. I choose to be happy every second of every day. I've learned that being happy is a choice. Sometimes work is mandatory, but you can choose to be happy while you're there. I've also learned to be more accepting of people and to let go of negative things more easily. Now that I have experienced loss, I know what I have, and my child and the people around me deserve to have positive encounters with me. I have learned to no longer waste my time and energy on those who have let me down.

Perhaps living emotionally broken and battered is not a bad thing at all. I may feel shattered at times, but my innermost light shines through the pieces. I think that by viewing the most shattering experiences as beautiful, the light shines through the cracks and gouges that have wounded us.

I feel like there have been so many people and things that

have helped me through hours, days, weeks, months and now years of healing. My daughter, of course, is my world, and I am the example that she must follow, so for her I keep my head up, my words kind and honest as possible. Sam's parents have been really inspiring. They are so caring and involved and I know there is an unspoken thing that happens when we gather; Sam is on all of our minds, he is with us. Sam's brother is like my brother, he's a wonderful uncle to Chanel and he has really turned his life around since this loss. I can see he had a deep awakening as well and I look forward to being witness to his successes in life.

I feel stronger these days. I feel as though I'm moving forward for the three of us. I now understand that my emotional intelligence is heightened. I also get the concept of compartmentalizing my pain, and emotionally dealing with each situation separately. I am capable of feeling more than pain.

I just became a homeowner and it was a good investment. It was difficult moving and uprooting from the place that Sam knew we were living. Removing ordinary items like glowing stars from my bedroom ceiling triggered a deluge of tears. He put those stars up for me with feeling! He was the last person to touch them. It just didn't feel right to remove them. I convinced myself, however that they were THINGS! Just THINGS, Kimberly! But the placement of those stars by Sam was a piece of my happiness. The items I inherited after his passing weren't as emotionally satisfying as these tiny glowing stars he intentionally placed on my ceiling. So, I've learned to appreciate Every, Little, Thing!

I knew the purchase of my home was the right thing to do. After I put in an offer I discovered that my new neighbor ironically turns out to be Sam's best friend. The purchase of this home was clearly meant to be; there's even a porch, perfectly ready for a swing. These incidental reminders of the life Sam and I planned are more valuable than gold, even if the connections are concocted in my own head. I hate that a small tote bag contains all that my daughter physically has left of her father. It isn't fair, but it is what it is. Life is comprised of small choices that determine the path to our future. Sometimes things just happen. That is where fate and daily happiness are created. I've become a more deeply spiritual person. I believe in an afterlife that doesn't seem so glum. I think it's possible that once you're dead you recover from the way you died and move onto more important things like learning your own soul and seeing its reflection more easily and readily in others. Before this tragedy, I took days, hell, even years for granted. Now there's a constant reminder to reflect on my time and behavior in a particular moment and consider: *am I absorbing all of life's available awesomeness? Am I putting forth all of my positive energy to create good memories and bonds with the ones I love? Am I being open to welcome love from new sources and people?*

Sometimes my happiness comes from doing nothing at all! I enjoy the brief hiatus of cutting myself off from the world to listen to the tune of my own soul. Sometimes I have to recognize just how small I am compared to the vastness of the universe and just enjoy the simple freedom to JUST BE. After losing Sam, I have come to many realizations about what is important in life and what isn't. I've learned to be happy for other people's successes; support those in need and no matter what, always do what I feel is right. It is my job to be the best woman and mother that I can be and I intend to do so with the best of my ability.

I have experienced happiness with my husband, have a great child and I feel fulfilled. I look forward to my life going as planned before. I am attending college, I am an entrepreneur, a traveler and a woman who is confident in herself and making the most of every day.

Two years after his passing, I asked Chanel what she remembered about her father. "I remember he colored with me and took me to the park," she responded.

There aren't an abundance of memories for her, so reflecting back to all the fighting I did to make him be an active participant and influence on her life helps me to better understand why he fought it. He often told me he would only live to be 27 or 28 years old. I would brush it off and tell him he was crazy for thinking that way. But, once again he was right. He had good intuition. I hope that other single parents get the message that forcing a parent to spend time or do extra things isn't productive; just be happy in what you do, that is the most positive message you can send a child. Anything else unexpectedly positive that happens is a bonus.

I struggled with my attachment to Sam for over a decade knowing there were toxic issues, but I forced the union anyway. This realization has changed me. I am now comfortable in letting people go who are not meant to stay and finally, I am able to cut attachments to relationships that are not mutually beneficial. Setting realistic goals for my life has helped make me make the most with my time instead of taking it for granted. I realize that I have gone through many situations that could have labeled me a victim, but I never saw myself as one and refuse to put myself in that category. Everyone has bad and painful experiences and the only thing that differs is how we process them. Grief, hurt, anger, and the sadness can make you open up and see the good side of things. I've learned to let the bad and questionable things go. What I choose to take from this is a whole new appreciation of life. I am also finding the balance of fulfilling the role of a father as a single mother. I have learned more about who I am and how to be there for others.

Because of my experiences with Sam I no longer question my instincts, I trust them. Although I am sad for him to have missed out on opportunities with his daughter, I am confident in my choices to keep her safe. My opinion of his daddy/daughter time may not have been popular with him and his friends, but thankfully, my daughter was not a witness during the murder of her father because of my strict expectations.

The courts recently gave our family an award through the witness advocacy program for exemplary behavior to the community choosing from over 700 families. But the award means a lot more to me because the group of people that loved Sam came together completely to serve the community with his dad leading the way. We are all new at this loss and growth process and we are going through it, for the first time, together. Sam's passing has bonded us together. Together and individually we miss him and that ache will not go away, until we too are missed.

I sit here almost two years later still picturing him laughing somewhere and then I remember that he's gone and my heart palpitates like its fresh news. I wonder what would have come of us. I still cry for him because there is no love like the love I gave to him. There is no other love like what I feel for Chanel and no other love like the love that he gave to us. That fact alone has forever changed me to continue to love in spite of the tragedy that was dealt us.

When my day comes, I hope his soul is there to greet mine with more knowledge so we can have a successful, happy, long, partnership to enjoy another life together.

Does heaven have a porch swing? If so, we'll be there.

No Excuses

Kimberly did a great job illustrating how situations can change at any minute. She took us on the journey with her while she learned to heal and learned to cope with the new circumstances life had handed her. When changes abruptly occur, sometimes it is hard to make sense of things and to move on. Sometimes these difficult situations become part of our identity. We try to move on but are constantly reminded of our painful past. It is fair to say that we have all experienced a few hurtful things in our past. It is also fair to say that we may feel that the hurtful things have left us at a disadvantage. You may feel that you do not come from a great socio economic background. You might not have grown up on "the right side of the tracks." You might feel that because of this or because of that you don't have the same opportunities as others.

I would like to introduce you to a young lady who holds a very dear spot in my heart. I have seen this girl grow and transform into the inspirational young lady she has become. She is a young lady who, I feel, could use any excuse as to why she was being held back or didn't have the opportunities to achieve much in her life. Even with the four inch scar down her wrist, she is no longer going to let her painful past define her.

Amy M.

I was only five when the adventures with my mom started. She woke me up one morning and told me to pack all my favorite things because we had a special day planned. As any five year old would, I packed Mrs. Dolly, all my stuffed animals, my favorite red shoes and my tutu. My mom came in and hastily packed more appropriate clothes and said that we could get the rest of the stuff on the road. I was so excited for this adventure! I had no idea where we were going or what we were doing, but my mom was so excited it made me excited too. All strapped into the car, we pulled out of the driveway and away from the last place I would ever know as home. That day my "adventures" with my mom began, but I later learned that it was just a massive game of hide and seek and I was the only one having fun.

The first day, we drove for what seemed to be forever, but in reality it was five hours to Santa Clara. We sang silly songs and played "I spy with my little eye" to pass the time and I napped a lot. When we got to Santa Clara we found a little room to sleep in. We arrived late in the night so as soon as we got into the room I tucked in Mrs. Dolly and kissed her good night then my mom did the same for me. The next morning we woke up and there was a roller coaster on the beach! Mom and I played all the games on the boardwalk, rode all the rides and ate everything my little tummy could hold. I loved this adventure and even won another stuffed toy to add to my group of friends that were with me. We stayed in Santa Clara for a little while, living life, and going on adventures.

One morning we woke up to loud banging on the door and my mom was so scared. She told me to pack everything and while she was calling the police, the banging continued. It was so loud and I didn't know why my mom was yelling at me because I was trying to pack everything, but I had to make sure the animals were all comfortable. I heard the police sirens and the banging stopped.

My mom gave me a hug and said, "I hope you liked this adventure," because she had another one planned for me. So we grabbed our stuff. I grabbed Mrs. Dolly and away from the little room on the beach we went.

We went from a little room on the beach, to a big house in San Francisco, to a shelter in Oregon, to a little hotel in Washington and I lost track after that. Each place we stayed for no longer than a few weeks, but each adventure with my mom was magical. Even though I never knew where we were going she always made it fun. There was always something new to explore or something new to learn. No matter where we were, I always had my mom, who was my best friend in addition to my animals, my tutu, red shoes and Mrs. Dolly. One day, "in a far off land" as I like to call it, we came back to our little room and the door had been broken in. We looked in the room and my tutu had been cut into little pieces, and there was stuffing from my animals everywhere. My mom had that scared look on her face and I knew that look meant this adventure was over and we were onto the next. We grabbed what we had left, what was left of my animals and got in the car. We drove for a little while and we stopped at a park. My mom got my stuffing-less animals out of the bag and she asked if I wanted to have a funeral. We could buy them flowers and tell stories about each one as we buried them. This was the first time I didn't want the adventures to go on anymore. I wanted to go back home to where we started. I wanted to go to where I first took my animals; where they and I were safe. I didn't want to go on anymore adventures. I cried as I told each animal goodbye and my mom held me close. She told me that we will lose things on the adventures but we would always have each other and as long as we were together, we were home.

For the next few years, my mom, Mrs. Dolly and my red shoes traveled about the country going from adventure to adventure. We would meet new friends and one day when I was 13, we stayed in one place. My mom said we would live here for a little while but to always stay ready for the next adventure. I had met new friends before but always knew that at any minute I would have to say goodbye, so I never really got close to anyone. This time I met a boy who became my friend. He was 15, a little older than me, but he was so sweet; he took me everywhere and introduced me to new people. I told him that I couldn't be his girlfriend because I didn't want to break his heart when the new adventure started. He laughed and said that was ok, he could just be my friend. It was nice to have a friend. I loved my mom and she was all I ever knew but it was really nice to have someone else to call a friend. On my 14th birthday, he gave me my first kiss, my stomach fluttered as there must have been 100 butterflies in there. He was so sweet he asked if he could hold my hand and at least be my boyfriend for the day. I had a boyfriend! That night we sat under the stars and talked about dreams and I fell asleep wrapped in his arms on the grass.

The next morning my mom brought us cereal and orange juice to have for breakfast on the lawn. He was so embarrassed and apologized for not having me back in the house at my curfew. She forgave him and reminded him in her sweet sarcastic tone to please be more respectful next time. After all, we were just in the backyard. After breakfast, I came inside with, what must have been, the biggest smile on my face. So big, in fact, that I completely missed that look on my mom's face which told me time and time again, it was time to go. I walked by her and noticed our stuff packed on the stairs. Without a word and tears pouring down my face I picked up the bags and went to put them in the car. Before I could reach the door, she grabbed my arm and asked if I was happy here. Through my tears I told her I was and with pain in her voice she said we could stay for a little longer in this town but we did need to leave this house. Leaving houses was nothing to me, I had moved houses so often that they just became a place to keep me out of the rain. The fact that I got to stay in the same town brought me so much joy. I jumped into her arms and knocked her tiny frame over. We did move into a new house that day but we stayed in that tiny town for a few more months. My own happiness; however, made me oblivious to the growing worry on my mother's face.

One afternoon I was watching TV and heard a knock at the door. My mom was in the kitchen and yelled for me to get it. I answered the door and a very tall man was standing there. He asked if I was Amy and when I said, "yes," he got this smile on his face that I had only seen people get when they were super happy. He said, "Amy, I am your dad."

I froze in the middle of the door way. *My dad?* I knew nothing about this man except that he didn't want to come on our adventures. I don't think it's possible to put into words all the feelings that were popping into my head. My dad was standing at the door. He asked if he could come in and talk to my mom as she came around the corner to see who was at the door. The moment she saw him I saw the look on her face that I had seen so many times before; it was time to go, no questions asked. I backed away from the door thinking I would just go pack my stuff as my mom began to cry and kept saying, "no, no, no," over and over again. He pushed his way into the house and ran at my mom. My mom screamed, "Amy RUN!" *This was my dad, scaring my mom and now hurting her?* She was all I had, my best friend. I did run but I ran at him. I grabbed him to try and pull him off. It was chaos, she was so scared, he was so angry, she just kept telling him she was sorry and pleading to not hurt her, to not hurt me. *What was my mom sorry for?*

I cried and screamed, "stop hurting my mom!" As I was hitting him, nothing helped. He threw his arms up which hit me in the face and knocked me back.

He took two steps back away from my mom, pulled a gun out and told her, "you will never leave me again!" Then boom, she was gone. My mom was shot, my mom was gone. I laid there where I had fallen, frozen, in shock. He turned to me and said he was sorry as he fired the gun at me, hitting my hip and within a second he turned and looked at my mom's lifeless body and shot himself in the chest. I laid there motionless, my mom was gone, from what I knew this man calling himself my dad was dead and I was left there to bleed to death. I wanted to die. I wanted to lay there and just bleed to death. I wanted to join my mom. I drifted asleep and woke up some time later in the hospital.

When I woke up there was a police officer sitting next to me and asked if he could ask me some questions. I thought, *the first thing when I wake up from a nightmare was someone asking if he could ask me questions?* I rolled over and I went back to sleep. The next time I woke up, there was a lady named Rachel, sitting on the edge of my bed. She introduced herself and asked if I knew what had happened. Of course I knew. I stared at her. She informed me that my mother was dead and my dad was expected to live. She told me, because of the circumstances of having no living family, she was going to be taking care of me. She then asked if I wanted to talk and I just screamed and cried, and the doctors gave me a shot to help me go back to sleep. *My mom was gone, all I had ever known, gone and now I am going to be taken care of by a person named Rachel.*

When I was well enough to leave the hospital Rachel took me back to the house to collect my things. When I walked back into the house I walked over to where my mom had died and laid down there and cried. Rachel told me I needed to get up and get my things but I just cried and cried. *What would I pack? Everything I wanted to take with me was lying on a slab in the basement of a hospital. There was nothing to pack. All I wanted, all I had was gone.* I laid on the blood stained carpet and just cried. When I got enough energy to get up, I walked up to my room looked around and grabbed the red of pair shoes that were now way too small for my feet and Mrs. Dolly and walked out. The funeral was a few days later. Rachel had taken me shopping for a dress and my boyfriend held my hand. I didn't say a single word. At the grave site they lowered her body and people threw dirt on her casket. People were throwing dirt on the one person I had ever loved and known! I broke my silence and screamed at everyone for their actions! I wanted to jump into the gaping hole with her. Rachel and my boyfriend held me down and back to the hospital I went.

A few days later, I woke up to Rachel talking to a smiling couple and the male half of the couple said, "she is kind of old but we will take her".

Rachel said, "It will just be temporary until we find you a baby."

This couple took Mrs. Dolly and me home with them that night. They showed me a cute little pink princess room and said this was my new place. I was 14 years old, not five, but I got into that pink princess bed and just cried. Later that night they asked if I wanted to come down for dinner. They told me they ate as a family and if I missed dinner I wouldn't eat that night. I went hungry that night and a few days after that. I was numb, in shock. Thoughts kept rumbling through my mind; *What if I didn't open that door? What if I didn't let him in? What if I knew what he had looked like? What if I knew why we were on adventures? What if I had known about our dismal game of hide and seek?* That moment was the first time I ever felt angry at my mom. *Why didn't she tell me the truth? I could have saved her if I had known!* I was also mad at God. *Why did I survive? Why did she die?* That night I walked down stairs for dinner, but I didn't eat, I only grabbed the steak knife off the table, hid it in my sweater and walked back to my room. I wanted to end my life and be with my mom. I went to the bathroom and sat in an empty bath tub. I took the knife and pressed it against my skin. I wanted to die but I was too much of a coward to even do that right. I learned that night, though, that when you place a blade against your skin and cut just a little, it takes away the emotional pain. That night I learned that I could just cut myself when I was sad and have a moment of being not so sad. That night I learned to cut.

After about two weeks of living with this couple they got their wish; a baby needed a house so I was no longer welcome. They walked me to the end of their driveway with Mrs. Dolly and my red shoes and said goodbye. As I drove off in Rachel's car, they hugged their new baby. This pattern continued for the next three years. I would stay in a house for no longer than a month, three months, if I was lucky. In three years I was in 15 different houses, 13 different cities each time replaced with a younger, cuter child. I learned there was no point in meeting new people or meeting new friends because I would just be shipped off to the next place. My story preceded me prior to each place I went. When I would get to a new school people would whisper, "that's the girl who killed her mom"; "That's the new girl, she's a foster kid." It was the occasional Christian club that would tell me they were sorry for my circumstance and befriend me out of pity. I hated life, and wanted to be dead with my mom. I was used to the constant travel and the new places to live but I always had my mom, my red shoes and Mrs. Dolly.

Four months before my 18th birthday Rachel sat me down and told me at 18 I would be on my own and she gave me a few flyers of places that could help me get a job and get me on my feet. I thought, *just like that at 18 you are no longer my responsibility and you will have to figure this world out alone.* In the same sentence she brought in my bags and informed me that the house I was living in once again needed me out and she had found a new home for me for the last few months of my "childhood". When I went through the very small bag of my belongings that they packed for me I noticed my red shoes were missing. I asked Rachel if she could take me back to the house to get the rest of my stuff and she informed me that all my things were in the bag. I let her know that my red shoes were not in there and she informed me they threw them away because they were too small and old and torn. She said it like it was nothing. Like they were nothing, like just an old pair of shoes. *Those were my dancing shoes that I would wear with my tutu and dance with my mom on each adventure. I was her tiny dancer and those were MY shoes.* I left the rest of my belongings in her office; I would no longer have use for them. I took only Mrs. Dolly and got into the new car of my next temporary stay.

This lady's name was Julie. She had a sweet voice but I had no idea what she said during the drive home. All I could think of was my missing shoes. It was almost like losing my mom all over again. They were not just a pair of shoes, they were a part of my mom, my journey and they were tossed away and had dirt thrown on them just like my mom. Julie walked me up to my new room and came back moments later with a tray of food for dinner. She wasn't going to make me eat with the family and was just trying to be nice. On the tray was a knife and I took it and walked to the bathroom. This time I didn't hesitate; I had the courage to push down thinking that this time I was going to cut as deep as I could and bleed out like my mom did. In four months I was going to be discarded and thrown to the wolves of this world anyway so I took that knife and cut three inches down my wrist. I was going to my mom, and in that moment of despair I was happy that I would see her again. Fortunately, Julie was a good foster mom and came up to talk to me and brought her food on a tray to eat with me. She didn't get her dinner that night because she called the ambulance and wrapped a towel around my arm. She started to cry and kept telling me, "don't you dare leave me! Stay with me!" I knew she meant that she didn't want me to die but after having been discarded so many times, hearing someone pleading for me to actually stay, might have given me a little energy not to die. I woke up with Julie and her husband Mike sitting at my bed. They were happy I wasn't dead. Julie jumped up and gave me a hug; I hadn't had a hug from anyone since the day my mom died. I looked over Julie's shoulder as she was hugging me and I saw Rachel. I pushed Julie off me and started to yell. I was mad she hugged me, *why would she show she cared just to give me back to Rachel?* I started to rip out my stitches as I thought life couldn't get any crueler than that moment right then. I watched my mom die, people kept discarding me and now a person acted like they cared just to turn around and do the same. I was sedated and strapped down to the bed. When I woke up this time they were all still there and Julie told me she was going to take me home and she wasn't going to get rid of me.

After my mandated suicide watch was over I went home with Julie and Mike. I wasn't allowed knives or scissors for a while, but I can understand their concern. It was nice for the first time feeling that someone was concerned for me, feeling that someone cared. As my 18th birthday neared, anxiety began to take over my mind. I had two weeks to figure life out, before I was just dropped and left to fend for myself. One day my high school principal called me into her office and told me that since I had changed schools so much I didn't have enough credits to graduate but I could take a test to get a GED and she felt that would be best considering I was going to be 18 soon. Not knowing exactly what "GED" meant, I understood her to say, "You're not good enough and when your 18 you are not a concern of mine anymore," (what I heard not what she said). I left her office and again didn't want to live anymore. I went home that night and planned that when Julie went to work in the morning, I would take my life. I knew if she was gone this time she wouldn't find me and save me. As she was leaving, she told me she wanted to talk to me when she got home and I just knew it was about me needing to leave her home. When I saw her car pull out of the driveway I grabbed two razors, in case I dropped one I would have a backup, and sat in the bathtub. I told my mom I would see her soon, and I used the scar from last time to guide my cut. When I was done I sat there happy that this life was over and that I would be dancing with my mom soon. I thought I would wake up in her arms but instead I woke up again, tied to a hospital bed with Julie sitting next to me. *I had failed again.*

Julie was crying and said she had forgotten her work keys and had come back home to find me passed out in a pool of my own blood. She thought that this time she had really lost me and I remembered thinking *who cares if you had lost me, you were getting rid of me in a two weeks anyways I just wanted to go out on my own terms.* She cried and said when I turned 18 she had hoped that I would want to stay with them; they wanted to help me figure things out and didn't want to see me go. If I chose to stay, I would have to see a counselor and I would have to go to college, but as long as I did that I was welcome to stay. She said she couldn't bear to see me in a bath tub of my own blood ever again. I didn't quite understand the generosity but I figured going to a counselor and college couldn't be worse than being alone and on my own.

My 18th birthday came and went with a celebration I will always remember. Julie made me a cake that was so black, my gothic heart was happy. I hadn't had a birthday cake in four years, and in these four years I don't even remember a birthday card. I am not sure in those four years if anyone, except Rachel, knew or cared when my birthday was. Julie did a great job showing me how a birthday should be celebrated. The next morning she told me we were going on an adventure. I don't think she knew what that word meant for me; I don't think she knew all the mixed emotions I would feel hearing those words. That word was a word of excitement and of pain. That word meant I would have to pack up and start over; that word meant my mom was scared, but I don't think Julie knew that. She told me to pack a small bag since we would be back the next morning. Adventures never meant we were coming back, adventures meant we were gone for good. Being 18 now and having my experience with adventure, I didn't know what to pack for a "we are coming back" adventure. Normally I would throw everything in a giant trash bag, grab Mrs. Dolly and walk to the car. I stood in my room a little confused and Julie instructed me to grab something to sleep in, a pair of clothes for tomorrow and things I would need for hygiene. She laughed and said, "you should probably take Mrs. Dolly too."

After we were packed for our "be back tomorrow adventure" we got in the car and drove off. It was the first time I felt peace with leaving. I actually trusted Julie and knew that tomorrow we would be back. We started off on our long journey and when I asked where we were going she just smiled and said you will see. We drove for three hours that day to a town I only remembered in my worst nightmares, to the town where my world had ended four years ago. We drove past the house of horror and I started to rock back in fourth in my seat as my head spun and my heart pounded through my chest. The car stopped at a park with headstones raised to the heavens. Julie got out of the car and I just sat there. I hadn't been to this place since my life was lowered into the ground. Julie looked into my motionless body and said, "I thought your mom would like to see you on your birthday too." I grabbed Mrs. Dolly and got out of the car. I walked over to the head stone that had my mom's name written on it and stood there. My mom wasn't there. This piece of rock that had her name on it was not my mom. My mom was cooking dinner in the house of horror, my mom was laughing on the roller coaster from the tiny room on the beach, and my mom was collecting sea shells and telling me all about their lives. My mom was not there but she was in my memory, in my heart and she as looking after me. She found Julie for me; when I realized my mom was not in the ground I turned to Julie and gave her a hug. The car ride home, I told Julie all about my mom. I shared all about her smile, love for life, all her joy, how we danced and how my mom always made sure I was taken care of first even if that meant she went hungry. My mom came alive for a minute as I shared her life with Julie and before I knew it, we did return to the house we left the day before. Julie was right.

Julie encouraged me to tell the counselor all the stories I had told her about my mom. She told me that the counselor would love to know who my mom was and share in those joys with me too. It felt good talking about my mom, it made me smile. The next time I went to counseling, I did share all the stories; Julie was right again, the counselor laughed with me and enjoyed learning about my mom. At the end of that session, the counselor said the words that I feel changed my life. She said, "it seems to me your mom did everything she could to keep you safe, keep you happy, and give you the best life she could." I definitely had to agree strongly with that statement, but then she continued. "With your mom looking down on you now, how do you think she would feel knowing you are trying to hurt yourself, knowing that you are trying to end your life? Your mom did everything she could to keep you alive and happy. Do you think your life now reflects what she wanted most for you? Do you feel that you are honoring your mom's wishes? Do you feel if you were to take your life, everything she tried to do for you would just be wasted?"

I had never thought of any of that. Here I was thinking, "poor me, no one wants me, I just want to be 12 and with my mom again." But yet, every game of hide and seek was her way of protecting me because she knew what kind of monster my "dad" was and she was protecting me from him. I did miss my mom dearly and she was the last I ever knew of love, but *would ending my own life mean that she died for nothing, that she ran for nothing?* I sat with that question burning a hole in my brain for a good week. *What would my mom want with my life?* She wanted me safe and she wanted me happy. For the first time I felt safe. I knew I could trust Julie. If she said something, I knew she meant it, so my mom got her wish of me being safe. *What did it look like to be happy? Happiness was with my mom. Happiness was dancing to the radio in tiny rooms, happiness was making pancakes shaped like Mickey Mouse.* I knew I couldn't have those moments back, but I knew I had to learn what happiness looked like at least for making my mom happy and giving her life meaning.

It has only been eight months since my 18th birthday. Seven months since the counselor had opened my eyes. It has been seven months since I have taken a razor to my skin and I know now that there is no happiness in causing pain. I am still learning what it means to be truly happy but I have a feeling I am not the only one still searching. I think the biggest shift came when I started looking for what happiness meant and I started to learn about myself. *What did I want to be when I grow up?* That was a question I never answered because I never imagined living long enough to grow up. *What were the things I enjoyed doing?* Again, something I never answered because I never cared to participate in anything; it was pointless, because at any minute I was off to the next place. Two very special people introduced me to the world of Jui Jitsu and showed me that no matter where I went, the sport was always there. I learned that physical exercise gave me the same high I sought out when I cut myself. Most importantly I learned to be who I wanted to be.

I was always the girl with the story, I was the girl who "killed her mom," I was the orphan; I was the weird, goth, suicidal foster child who wouldn't graduate high school. I was the girl who had no friends, the girl no one cared about, the girl who was better off dead. Those labels were heavy and I thought they were how I was identified. To Rachel and all my other foster homes, I was #228578, just a number. I didn't want to be that girl. I didn't yet know who I was, but I did know that I didn't want to be her. I didn't have to forget my past or forget my mom, but I had to stop living in it. I had to stop telling people who I was by the story of my youth and had to start telling them who I was going to be. I didn't know how to make friends but, thanks to Facebook, I met three people who actually care about me and with their help and Julie's, I began to define who I wanted to be. I gained confidence that I have a future and if not to the whole world, I mean something to these four people and my mom. Feeling like I had some sort of value, I spoke with my counselor and asked how I could get a job doing what Rachel did or if there was a job I could be of importance to a child who feels thrown out, who feels how I felt. *I knew firsthand that feeling and I wanted to try to help other children.*

I know I have a long road ahead of me, but that's the exciting part; it is a head of me and not behind me. My future is what I make of it and isn't defined by my past. I am not an orphan, I am a college student. I didn't kill my mom, my "dad" did. I may have scars on my wrist but now they are a reminder of how far I have come. I may still be the weird goth girl but that's because I choose to be. I will live this life as my mom had hoped for me. I am not my past. I am what I choose to be now and in the future. And as for Mrs. Dolly, well she is there to cheer me on!

You Are YOU

I like how she said, "I have my whole life in front of me." Amy chooses to see her life for what it could be instead of what it was. She decided she wasn't going to let the false labels affect her anymore. We have to let go of things in our past that no longer serve us. We have to choose to let go of our hurts and our pains, forgive others and forgive ourselves. We need to drop the heavy baggage that slows or even stops our growth.

This next story brings our journey full circle. No matter what happens in our lives we define who we are and what we are going to be. Our next author comes to the realization that life may be shorter than expected. She discovers what matters most in life and above all boldly defines who she wants to be and exactly how her life will be lived.

Emma Borders

Life was amazing (and straight out of a CW show): frat parties and beach life, college cheerleading, late night pizza, meeting the boy of my dreams and getting engaged. In 2007, life was easy. I was a 21 year old, regular chick, finishing up my 4th year of college in Southern California, half way through my second BA, on my way to graduating with honors for film editing. I had a great job, coaching figure skating which funded my shopping habit and Starbucks addiction and was living with my other cheerleader/dancing friends on the Newport Beach peninsula. I felt like I was a live version of Elle Woods with blonde ambition and living the So Cal dream. I was fiercely independent, completely motivated and I was ready to take on the world and the world was just waiting for me to ripen. I was planning my wedding and the future seemed so tangible and so real. Just one more year - just one more until the life I had always imagined past graduation was about to start - "real life," and oh boy did it get real.

It began with my pinky finger going numb, which, after moving brand new furniture into my very first apartment with my fiancé, did not seem strange - *probably a pinched nerve* I told myself. The bump in my arm pit that followed was not that alarming either. All the weird ailments of dorm living, gross coed's, and stress had made me a little less weary of every bump and bruise. Three weeks later and no improvement, I reluctantly dragged myself to the student health center to get my Z pack of antibiotics for what they thought was either a shaving infection or clogged pore. The lump's resilience seemed to dumbfound not only me, but the staff of doctors who blindly handed out antibiotics like they could cure the world. (...or at least that week's STD). Fast forward four months later, strep tests, ruling out mono, multiple x rays, mammograms, ultra sounds, blood tests, and finally, full blown surgery to biopsy nine lymph nodes, concluded with a two week period of waiting while my surgeon went on vacation. I wouldn't say I was a glass half empty kind of girl, but I always tried to be realistic about the odds of any situation and numbly knew that the results might not be in my favor despite the rainbows and unicorns my friends and family nervously tried to stuff down my throat in anticipation. When waiting on the precipice of life-changing news, I was oddly calm, perhaps in shock, while everyone around me created a bubble of denial, which is probably why I faced my verdict in solitude. Without the dramatics, I was told in very matter of fact way that I had Non Hodgkin's Lymphoma in the second stage.

I had cancer.

I had cancer at 21. *What does that even mean?!* "I have cancer." I kept repeating in my head as I sat in the oncologist's waiting room later that afternoon by myself amongst the several geriatric chemo patients drooling all over themselves. It did not seem real and my oncologist consulted me as if I had something as straightforward and mundane as a common cold. "You will do this, this, this, and this, oh and this by next week," he said, as if surgery for port catheters, and lumbar punctures, and pet scans, and echo cardiograms were a normal part of my every day check list.

"What happens if I don't?" I asked, as if I had a choice.

"You won't make it another year." He said flatly.

Okay then! And that was settled.

Cancer became another college class, with homework assignments, and meetings and I just did whatever I was told and on time so that I could pass this one with an "A" as well.

Seven days after the C word came crashing down upon me, I was getting stabbed in the chest at the worst happy hour ever so the cocktail of wonder drugs could access my port. For those unfamiliar with a port - the chemical poison is often so toxic that it will eat away at the skin surrounding a normal IV. Chemotherapy, after all, was inspired by napalm from the Vietnam War. To prevent this adverse reaction, a hollow ping pong ball shaped device is surgically placed under the skin and attached to a tube that is woven into the heart cavity so that the "medicine" can immediately be distributed into one's blood system. Mine was a closed device, so the skin of my chest completely covered it and was accessed by popping the skin and the ping pong ball with a rather large gagged needle, usually by the most inexperienced nurse since I was the youngest, least fragile patient in the row of BarcaLoungers...

Being sedated and on cloud 9 after my first round of treatment, I convinced my Dad I was starving and needed Panera on the ride home, only to learn about the awesome side effects a few hours later when I met my friend, the porcelain God, and discovered what broccoli cheddar soup looks like on the return trip. The throne and I became great friends - great friends for the next eight months... My Cliff's notes version of chemotherapy is that it is the world's worst and longest hangover. I would drive around to school, work, doctor appointments, wherever, with a big gulp sized cup because I could not go any amount of distance or time without having to empty my stomach - even if nothing was in it. They said that if I had been middle aged alcoholic man that my system would have handled the drugs better. (I guess all the frat parties and "jungle juice" just didn't do the job!) So instead we tried every prescription anti-nausea medication out there, including a synthetic weed in pill form which they did not educate me of until I took it for the first time trying to lead a Baby Blades ice skating class. Trust me, at that point of feeling like gunk, the last thing you need is to be is high and teaching two year olds! I taught ice skating and continued to go to school throughout treatment because what else was I going to do? Stay at home? I thought to myself, honestly, how big of a pity party are you going to throw yourself and there's really not that much *Grey's Anatomy* to watch anyways.

My hair fell out four weeks earlier than expected and the very expensive extensions I was trying out for our wedding did not have time to be removed properly while chunks were falling from my scalp. So I made the big girl decision to pull them (and my hair out) from the root and my fiancé helped me Bic my head... It was another numb surreal moment in the long process that was the big C. I felt ugly and completely alien. As teenagers and young adults, thanks to raging hormones and insecurities, we all feel as if we don't belong and I, like everyone else, just wanted to blend. I struggled wearing my issues on the outside like a big fat scarlet letter; not even be able to hide behind a good hair cut and blow out, which had been my previous prescription for self loathing. In the never ending love hate relationship a girl has with her hair, I NEVER imagined I would ever have to go without it completely. It felt like I was losing part of my identity and it all happened so fast that I could not deny I was becoming THE CANCER PATIENT and no longer myself, practically overnight I bought a long blonde wig and in a moment of trying to laugh at myself, lovingly named her Shaniqua. Even trying to muster courage through the irony of my inside joke, I instantaneously felt ridiculous and that I was fooling no one. Although, what I discovered during treatment is that the general population is so self involved that most people don't even notice or care about things that we, especially women, obsess about and that I really was creating an issue that mattered to no one other than me. Most of my classmates did not even realize anything was different let alone that I was sick. My vanity and ego had to be checked at the door for several years and as a 20 something retired cheerleader about to get married, it was a lesson I struggled with deeply. From scans, I knew my body was responding to the treatment, but it didn't feel like my body. It was hard to believe I was "winning" when I was physically deflated, fat, weak, and a sick shade of green. I was so pathetic that even walking across a parking lot to my car was difficult. The oncologist had me pumped full of steroids to counteract this reaction which then in turn ballooned me up 30 lbs on my 5'4" frame. The steroids caused full blown face and body acne that just about put me over the edge, let alone all the side effects than did not alter my external appearance. And worse, from thousands of deep conversations with my fiancé, I now knew that I was no longer attractive to him... as if I didn't already know. *How could I be so vain when I was lucky just to live?* As a Gemini, I already knew I had multiple personalities and was probably teetering on the edge of crazy when healthy; but the internal battle of just being alive vs. not being satisfied with what remains to live, was mentally and emotionally exhausting and made me feel guilty on top of everything else.

Life was miserable. I wished away the year and wanted nothing but to crawl in a hole and endure as much of the labor of cancer on my own. I hated being the cancer patient. I hated being pitied and did not want to lose my independence. I didn't even let my parents come visit often because their biological desire to take care of me felt like smothering even though they were only trying to help. At this point I was 22, I was supposed to be an adult. I was supposed to be a full functioning part of society and here I was barely functioning, period. I started reaching out to old and new friends just to feel connected to anything and discovered that I was only the cancer to them - no longer "me," but a huge representation of their own fears of mortality. They were either scared to see me, talk to me, or completely opposite - verbally vomited all over me. Once people knew I did not have a genetic disease, that it was environmental, I could see the panic in their eyes when they asked how I contracted it as if it as if I purposely slept in a bed of asbestos. I did nothing other than live my life just like everyone else. I was a non smoker, non alcoholic, non drug user, and avoided fast food as much as possible. I don't know why I was a chosen one. I did not and still don't blame them for their fear, but their tact made me feel like such a leper. One popular opinion was that I "contracted" it from overdoing it in college. If that was the case, every stressed out coed would be a member of the walking dead (...well, maybe some are.) Some told me it was because I wasn't vegan, or the water in my home town, others told me it was God's plan. At Thanksgiving that year, my absentee aunt who I only saw or spoke to during the holidays, sat me down and asked me what I thought I did to give myself cancer because God did not give me this disease. I was never hateful of my path just wary of my fate and I felt so isolated from my former life because few people could still just accept me and not put me and my situation down. At a family BBQ, my soon to be sister-in-law asked me what the percentages of survival were.

"I was given an 80% chance of living to see age 27, even with treatment," I said.

"But we could all get hit by a car tomorrow" she rebutted. The fight to argue with her wasn't worth it.

"Okay, you win... we can all die tomorrow," I replied.

According to the National Safety Council, we have a 1 in 112 chance of dying in a motor accident, a 1 in 136,011 chance of dying by lightening…I still have been told that I have a 20% chance of dying now. NOW. Not in a hypothetical car accident. People in their 20's don't realistically want to think about death. Especially not the possibility that tomorrow is not a given. To young adults, there is a false sense that we are invincible - we are the future - we have our whole lives ahead of us to make stupid decisions and still take over the world! But what if we don't?

I was a lucky one this time around. My body did what it was supposed to and the poison, I mean chemotherapy, worked. Six months into the recovery process my scans showed clear, but in the oncology world, the insurance on a cancer prognosis is to go a few more rounds to make sure you got it all, even if it kills you in the process. It was at that point I got angry. I could see a light at the end of the tunnel. I was not going to die but it was hard to celebrate because I still looked and felt like a cancer patient and was anxious to move past it all. I wanted to go back to being *me*. I had a wedding to plan and a dress to fit into!

Almost a year after D Day, I was weak, fat, bald and had the stamina of a snail. I was embarrassingly falling asleep anywhere I went because everything was exhausting. To fight back, I focused on getting back in shape so I could "re-enter" the general population and maybe save some face with my college life before graduation. Working out was a slow process - one step at a time. Literally step by step on the treadmill. A mile was a phone home occasion. The marathon Barbies sprinting for hours next to me made me feel ridiculous since the competitive nature in me couldn't keep up, but they also secretly motivated me to work off the toxic pounds as quickly as possible. It was watching these turbo women that made me realize that strong is sexy and it gave me something to aspire to! Wearing head wraps to the gym made me the target of everyone's gaze, but it was then I started to develop and own my Zena Cancer Warrior Princess attitude because there was no way to hide from the attention. Though I was starting to own my illness and celebrate survivorship, I desperately wanted my hair back. That August, I got that married in Shaniqua and went into debt trying to keep up that high maintenance bimbo. (Real hair wigs cost upwards of $2000 and having her attached to the little hair I was growing back was a couple hundred each time.) Shaniqua had literally taken on a persona of her own by that point. When the day came nearly a year later to ditch her, I didn't feel ready to reveal the peach fuzz that was my real hair, but I needed to stop hiding. The kids at the ice skating rink felt compelled to blabber to my face, as kids do, that I was ugly… Awesome guys. I love you too.

I found solace in working out. It was something proactive and healthy that I could do on my own and most importantly, because I COULD. At that moment, I was no longer dying and had no excuse not to start living. It is very common though with Non Hodgkin's to relapse around two years and I didn't want to sit around waiting for the ominous C to come back and ruin my life. After the wedding I needed something new to obsess about and came across a website for the Leukemia and Lymphoma Society's (LLS) Team in Training (TEAM), a fundraising charity group that taught participants how to run half and full marathons. At the time, 2 miles was a joke for me to even fathom. I don't know how I convinced my husband to commit to raising $6000 for LLS with me and both "run" our very first half marathons (13.1 miles). In retrospect, I call it my "cancer high"...That darn thing has gotten me into far too much trouble! TEAM was amazing. I was finally among a group of random, like-minded individuals who gave a damn that I was alive and running alongside them. Most of them were running in memory or in honor of a loved one who passed away from or survived the same disease. I was neither good at running nor fast, but I was stubborn and persistent. It seemed really cool to try something I would have never even attempted before I was sick, especially while doing something good for others through charity fundraising (which, I'm embarrassed to admit, is also something I probably would not have done before I was sick). We did "run" our first FULL marathon (26.2 miles) that season and signed up for the next... My husband and I worked our way from participants, to mentors to assistant coaches over several seasons and my most important roll became honored teammate - being the face to this ugly disease and getting to share my story for awareness. It was very therapeutic and it made the anxiety of all the many blood work appointments and scans easier because I knew if I did relapse, that I would have a support system this time. At some point we transitioned with marathon friends to the triathlon team (swimming, biking, and running). Trust me, still being a chubby 20 something, learning to swim and ride a bike in tight spandex was humbling, but forced us all to let down our guards so much quicker. My team of triathlon friends is some of the closest real life friends that I've ever had. Along the way, my "cancer high" saved me through the terrors of open water swims and emotional break downs, trying to get my bike up a dang mountain. Triathlon is my therapy because never in a thousand years did I ever imagine that my dance, ice skating or cheerleading background would ever lead me to such a blood, sweat, and gut grueling sport. Then again, I never in a thousand years thought that I would ever hear the words, "You have cancer." Throughout the evolution of learning that impossible is just a limit we put upon ourselves, I was introduced to Ironman.

People who do Ironman are not human and definitely not sane. The 140.6 mile race is composed of a 2.4 mile swim, 112 mile bike ride, and 26.2 mile run within a 17 hour time limit. Less than .002 percent of the population can call themselves Ironman. After time, the tick of Ironman got stuck in my brain. I signed up with 10 other friends one year out (with no refunds) for our first full Ironman. The journey getting there, 100 mile bike rides, ocean swims, 3 hour training days…every day…most by yourself, made me strong mentally and physically and mostly emotionally. During that year of training, a beloved TEAM staff member secretly fought and lost her battle with breast cancer. The loss was terrible, I wept at her funeral wondering why she, loved by thousands, with three kids who need her, was "chosen" to leave this world and not I. It made no sense then. It still makes no sense. I will never be healed from this experience or ever understand or even comprehend why. Her children will never know their mother, but me - just little me got a second chance. Maybe pushing myself in these races is a way to understand a way to revisit the discomfort of not knowing the outcome of cancer, that life is not always pretty or predictable; to experience the highs because of the lows. Doing an Ironman was not a justification of being "chosen" to stay in this world, but a way to redefine what being alive meant, going to the brink of possibility and hopefully surviving (or die trying). Only in retrospect do I understand that Ironman was a metaphor for the journey of dying and making it through the other side, but with Ironman, the grit, pain, and glory would be on my terms.

Only five years after attempting my first two mile run and 12 months of focused intense training, I completed the 2013 Ironman Coeur d'Alene, with my husband by my side, in 16 hours 47 minutes. Only 13 minutes to spare. That day, I pushed it to the brink - I felt strong, I felt weak, I wanted to cry, I wanted to scream - but I felt alive. It was my five year "cancerversary" that month. In the cancer world, five years is the Mecca. If you can make it that long, you've got a chance. Hell of a way to celebrate. We went on to finish Ironman Arizona in November of 2014 and will hopefully cross the finish line in Tennessee in 2015. I will never be able to feel satisfied or at peace with the big C and with racing, and I will continue to strive for what is next in search of some closure.

What I do know is that when I started training for Ironman, all of a sudden, I didn't want to know or have the OCD need to know if my blood was clear... F*CK it - if its back it can wait - I've trained too hard for this to let cancer take this from me too... Pretty irresponsible I know. Since the five year mark, scheduling blood tests has been left to my discretion. Between the early frequent tests, I used to fear that every little ache or fatigue was a sign it was back. Since Ironman, the most liberating realization has been that I could live life without the fear as a part of my daily life, that I could let it go and just accept it and redirect my energy. I even sent Shaniqua to wonderful to fiery death. Cancer will always be a part of me. Cancer is a part of me. I have the date I was diagnosed tattooed on my forearm as a reminder of how the world stopped turning that day and that I remain here on borrowed time... In a long roundabout way it dictated my life, what job I could keep and where I lived. It tested my relationship with my husband and made us stronger in the end for it. It dictated my hobbies, the friends I keep, the things I hope to accomplish in case it relapses, directs my life. Heck, I may never have children because of it. I am not ashamed and I try not to be obsessive. I love the path that we have found since this disease redirected everything I had planned and I cannot imagine what life would be without having experienced it. Yet, finally, almost eight years later, I find myself not needing to be recognized as the cancer patient anymore because I now would rather be known as strong...I am Ironman... I am Emma.

Conclusion

"I am Emma" is such a powerful statement! She is who she wants to be. Emma defines herself! She didn't say "I am a cancer survivor." Yes, she did survive cancer, and we are all thankful she did, but that isn't how she decided to define herself. In fact, none of the authors of these stories are defined by their circumstances. Ashley survived abuse, but she isn't an abuse victim. She is a mother, a powerful, strong, confident woman who now helps others who were once in her shoes. Deborah is not an amputee, she is a woman who lives life to the fullest and swims in the ocean and strives to empower others. Kimberly's sudden loss will always be a part of her story but she continues to strive for her dreams, takes care of her daughter and will always follow her instincts. Christine doesn't define herself by the life altering health setbacks, she is a mother and a wife still chasing after her dreams. These ladies define who they are; their circumstances do not.

These stories are mere moments in time in a long road of life. They comprise of seconds compared to the whole journey. Any of us could have stopped, thrown in the towel and let the circumstance define us, but this wasn't the end game for any of us. We all wanted to live, to be victorious. We wanted life and life abundant.

There are circumstances that may detour your direction. There may even be things that hinder you from even starting the journey. You may not even have a car to get on the highway of life. Your journey looks impossible without a car, but you can always walk along the road, or find a friend willing to give you a lift. Don't let that moment be what defines you or your journey. Don't let the failure, or the set back or the detour be what stands in your way. Don't let those moments become the labels of your life. This is your life; YOU choose who you are. YOU choose the destination. It is *you* who defines *you*. I wanted to be a champion. I didn't want to sit on the side lines. I could have said, "I was doing my best but an injury stopped me," or, "I am not letting this moment define me and I am going to achieve my goals." When I am older I can honestly look back at my life and say I gave it my all. All of us can.

Andrea literally risked everything to achieve her dream and now has a little human calling her a mom. Amy P. gets to hold her baby because she never gave up and thanks God for answering her prayers. Amy M. lives an inspiring life because she realized her mother's goal for her and never gave up.

None of these stories are over. They are a glimpse into the ongoing victories of today. We all must make choices every single day to continue to live the life we want. Tiffany gets to choose to respect her husband and set an example for her children. Ashley must daily redirect the focus of her life to her goals. The victories shared in these stories are victories for today.

We hope that you can see the possibility for victory in your own life beyond all the obstacles and challenges. If you desire victory in your own life and you stop at nothing to get it, you will attain it. Choose the path you want to be on. Do not let anyone tell you that you can't achieve something because of a label they have placed on you! I have said this before, but YOU define you. I know life's situations have tried to label you but only *you* can accept or refuse those labels. ONLY YOU DEFINE YOU!

So let's start today. ***Who do you want to be?*** Right here, right now, no matter the circumstance, choose who that person is and decide to be that person. Do you want to be the optimist or the pessimist? Do you want to be happy and content or angry and bitter? Do you want to be fearful or hopeful? No matter what your circumstances are, the choice is yours and yours alone. Start today by defining who you are and begin your journey to the winners circle! What can you do today to begin the life affirming walk to the winner's circle? The journey won't be smooth but weather the storms and enjoy the sunshine. Starting today, you can celebrate the little victory of the day. Day by day celebrating victories will start to add up and life will become a celebration! One day, you too will victoriously join hands with us and stand proudly in the Winners' Circle!

Resources

All the ladies are here to offer support. Feel free to reach out to any of us at www.JenaeNoonan.com on the contact page. For help and specific resources, we have included the below list of references.

Non Profit Organizations

Stay Safe, LLC. - *www.staysafeedu.com*

Team in Training - *www.teamintraining.org*

Leukemia and Lymphoma Society - *www.lls.org*

American Cancer Society - *www.cancer.org*

Health and Wellness

Suicide hotline - *(800) 273-8255*

CAF Challenged Athletes Foundation San Diego, CA

www.challengedathletes.org

SCP Southern California Prosthetics Irvine, Ca. - www.*scprosthetics.com*

Domestic Disputes

Battered Womens' Shelter - *www.safepassagelives.org*

Domestic Violence Hotline - *www.thehotline.org*   *(800) 799- 7233*

Child Protective Services Hotline - *(800) 422-4453*

Relationship

Married 4 Keeps - http://greatnonprofits.org/orgA/married-4-keeps

Unveiled Wife - www.unveiledwife.com

Finances

Ron Siegle - *http://wwwSiegelLendingTeam.com*

Dave Ramsey - *www.daveramsey.com*

Money Saving Mom - *www.moneysavingmom.com*

Substance Abuse

Alcoholics Anonymous - *www.aa.org*

Al-Anon - *www.al-anon.org*

Celebrate Recovery - *http://www.celebraterecovery.com/*

Family

Adopt Us Kids - *http://www.adoptuskids.org/for-families/how-to-foster*

www.ingramcontent.com/pod-product-compliance
Lightning Source LLC
Chambersburg PA
CBHW051948090426
42741CB00008B/1314